I

————————

Mondrala Press wishes to thank all its friends, fans, patrons, and investors for making this book possible, and especially:

Ms. Randa Dumanian
Mr. and Mrs. Karol and Dagmara Maziukiewicz
de domo Sowul

without whose enthusiasm and open hearts this book
could never have happened.

————————

ALEKSANDER'S ANTIQUITIES

A MEETING IN OEA

OR, CONCERNING PLATO

by Aleksander Krawczuk

translated by Tom Pinch

SECOND EDITION

MONDRALA PRESS

Originally published in Polish in 1970 as
Pan i jego filozof. Rzecz o Platonie.

Editing by Mondrala Press
Cover Design Mondrala Press

ISBN eBook: 978-2-919820-37-5
ISBN paperback: 978-2-919820-38-2
ISBN hardcover: 978-2-919820-39-9

The frontispiece illustration is by Maurice François Alfred Martin van Miële (1893-
1926) ("Martin van Maële") from Apuleius (transl. Jean de Montlyard), L'*Âne d'or*,
Charles Carrington, Paris, 1905.
The illustrations inside the text are by Jean de Bosschère (1878-1953), a Belgian
author and illustrator, who illustrated the 1925 Bodley Head limited edition of
Apuleius's
Golden Asse.

Isis appears to Lucius (or... to Apuleius on the shores of Corinth?)

TRANSLATOR'S SPECIAL REQUEST
Translating and publishing this book has been a labor of love for me.
I grew up reading it, and I have always wanted to be able
to share it with my American friends. And so here it is.
It will not make me rich, but if you liked the book, would you please
recommend it to a friend?
And give it an Amazon review?
https://www.amazon.com/dp/2919820494

THANK YOU!

TABLE OF CONTENTS

A MEETING
IN OEA

A MEETING IN OEA

Whether it was chance that brought me to this city, to Oea,[1] or fate, I cannot say. I sigh: "May I never have set foot here!" But the respect I owe my wife forbids such thoughts.

I, Apuleius of Madauros,[2] was on my way to study in Alexandria. I took the land route along the sea coast: from Carthage straight to Hadrumetum and Thapsus, then turned east at Little Sirte, then through Sabratha to Oea. And I got stuck here. A long and arduous journey still awaited me: the shores of Great Sirte, then the cities of Cyrenaica, a good chunk of wasteland beyond, and only then Alexandria.

But I got stuck in Oea. And in the winter, too, when it is best to travel in these parts because it is cooler. Wearied with my journey, I found hospitality at the house of my friends, the Appius family, and I took to bed at once, exhausted by illness. Looking back on the matter now, I do wonder at the cause of my weakness.

After several days, Pontianus visited me while I was still very sick. He had recently returned from Rome, and I was to learn only much later what had caused him to leave the capital and return to his hometown, a very nice town but well in the back of beyond.

I had met Pontianus through mutual acquaintances a few

---

[1] Modern Tripolis in Libya.

[2] A Berber-Roman city in Africa. The ruins of Madauros lie close to M'Daourouch in modern Algeria.

years ago during my studies in Athens. Soon we became close friends. And now, in Oea, Pontianus treated me with great deference (indeed, he was younger, though not much). He looked after my health and showed me a lot of solicitude. I now know where all that had come from.

First, he began to suss out my intentions and willingness, but carefully and evasively. He saw at once that I was eager to continue my journey and that other concerns were far from my mind: all I really desired was to study the secret teachings of Egypt, as divine Plato had done five hundred years ago and Pythagoras before him. In order to delay me, he began to assure me that if I only stayed in Oea for a while until he was ready, we could travel together. He also argued that I had already lost this winter season due to my illness, so I had to wait for the next winter because it was difficult to cross the Great Sirte in the summer: it was hot, and there were too many dangerous beasts, especially poisonous snakes.

These were sensible arguments, and I allowed myself to be persuaded. I was still weak, the season was indeed late, and the prospect of making a long journey in the company of such a dear friend seemed enticing. But where was I to dwell while I waited for the coming of winter? It couldn't possibly abuse the hospitality of the Appiuses forever. Pontianus immediately found counsel:

"You'll move to my mother's house. We will welcome you with joy. We have enough space. The apartment is very healthy, and the building is located so conveniently that you will be able to enjoy the view of the sea."

Who knows if my doubts were not outweighed by this last argument, for I know nothing quite so wonderful as that unfathomable view of the expanse of the sea not to be encompassed with the eye, especially when the moon rises above it. At such times, there comes before my eyes the wonderful apparition which I have once seen on a moonlit spring night far away, on the coast near Corinth.

So, as soon as I had the strength, I stood before the house of Pudentilla, Pontianus's mother. I was there to introduce myself.

ABOUT APULEIUS

Before our narrator finds himself in front of the lady of the house, we should briefly interrupt the flow of our story in order to introduce him to our reader.

Apuleius was born around 125 AD in the city of Madauros, in what is now Algeria, near its border with Tunisia, and which then lay in the Roman province of Africa Proconsularis. As a young and relatively wealthy man, he traveled a lot. He studied in Athens and Rome and later became very famous thanks to his writings. His novel *Metamorphoses,* also known as *The Golden Ass,* proved a huge bestseller. It was read with delight both in antiquity and in the Middle Ages. It has since been translated into almost all European languages. The concept is excellent: a young man accidentally and through no fault of his own is turned into a donkey; he experiences many tragicomic adventures until finally, by the favor of the goddess Isis, he regains his human form. Into the plot, Apuleius interwove numerous short stories, so the whole work is rich and varied. There are realistic chapters and fairy tales, erotic tales and adventure plots, and even sublime and religious themes.

We should note that Apuleius did not invent this man-and-ass story. He based his work on a certain Greek romance, an abridged version of which, also in Greek, has been preserved down to our times in the collection of Lucian's writings.[3] But Apuleius paraphrased it brilliantly, and he enriched the novel with many autobiographical elements, especially in those parts concerning the goddess Isis. Yet, *The Metamorphoses* is not a truly original work. The idea is someone else's; Apuleius's own is only its style, which is unusual and very charming.

And his other writings? There were a lot of them, and not all of them survived down to our times. *Florida* has a strictly literary and

---

[3] Lucian of Samosata (c. 125 – after 180) was a Hellenized Syrian satirist, rhetorician and pamphleteer who is best known for his characteristic tongue-in-cheek style, with which he frequently ridiculed superstition, religious practices, and belief in the paranormal.

rhetorical character: it is a selection of finer excerpts from speeches that Apuleius delivered on various occasions. Their style is that of a virtuoso, but they are trivial in content.

Finally, we have three short philosophical treatises by the same author. One is almost certainly no more than the Latin translation of a treatise attributed to Aristotle. Two others are more independent. One ponders the topic of Socrates' guardian spirit. The other presents the life and views of Plato.

Although this last work is a bit superficial, it testifies to the almost religious cult that Apuleius, a pupil of the Athenian Academy, had for its founder. It is the oldest exposition of Platonic philosophy in Latin, and for this reason, it will always have its place in the history of our culture.

And finally, there is his most personal work, and therefore, in a way, the most important: *The Apology*, or *Defense*. Whom was Apuleius defending? Why, himself! And against what? The patient reader of this book will easily guess it in the course of our story, which is largely based on *The Apology*. The reader should be forewarned, however, that this is neither a translation nor even a paraphrase of *The Apology*, for we freely transformed and enriched its material with various elements from other sources. In this way, we think we created a certain whole, which gives a somewhat surprising yet authentic picture of the customs and mentality of the educated classes during the heyday of the Roman Empire.

What a bizarre mixture of contradictions we find in one and the same man! Subtle intelligence and vast knowledge coexist with the downright superstitious cult of sorcery and magic. And at the same time, this philosopher and adept of the secret sciences shows cold self-interest and amazing sobriety in everything that concerns matters of property.

Perhaps, however, this mixture of contradictions is not something unusual or peculiar only to those times. If you think about it and look around, it would probably not be difficult to identify people in every era who were intelligent, learned, calculating, and at the same time, timidly paying homage to the most obvious nonsense and delusions. In the final analysis, it seems that each age is best characterized by its follies, superstitions, psychoses, and diseases; the idols of every epoch become the object of the ridicule and derision of the epochs that follow, which are not less bizarre, just bizarre differently.

The setting for Apuleius' adventures described in this book is Oea, today's Tripoli in Libya. The adventures of our illustrious hero in that city constitute one thread of the book. The second thread concerns much earlier times, takes place elsewhere, and discusses completely different issues. The two threads are connected by the person of Apuleius. We will exploit the fact that he had serious philosophical interests and assume that it was in Oea that he collected materials for his treatise on Plato. We will try to draw as realistic a picture of the man as possible, though we can't always be sure that he would have subscribed to all the comments and reflections we put in his mouth.

It is best, however, that we let him speak. We left him knocking on Pudentilla's door.

PUDENTILLA AND THE POEMS OF PLATO

She was probably forty and, therefore, about ten years older than me. At first glance, she seemed to me a woman of quite average beauty. Based on the expression on her face, I sensed that she was rather strict with herself and others, independent-minded, and willful. And little wonder: she'd been widowed for many years, lived alone, and was in charge of a large estate and of bringing up two sons: Pontianus, about whom I have already spoken, and Pudens, who was much younger, still a boy.

In the course of a very pleasant conversation, it turned out that Pudentilla was well-read and intelligent. She spoke Greek perfectly, perhaps even more fluently than Latin. In this part of the country, it is not something exceptional because a lot of Hellenes have always lived here.

Speaking of languages: I was surprised to note that in Oea, just as in my country, near Madauros, one still met people, especially in the countryside, whose mother tongue was Punic. This was obviously an inheritance from the ancient Phoenician settlers, a left-over of the Carthaginian rule that had once stretched all the way from Madauros in the west as far as Leptis in the east over everything that is today our province of Africa Proconsularis. I noticed that even the very young Pudens, introduced to me at the beginning of our meeting, preferred to speak Punic rather than Latin—and he mauled his Latin unbearably, by the way. Apparently, the boy had spent his childhood in the countryside. And yet old Punic Carthage had been destroyed down to its foundations over three hundred years ago, and today—great and magnificent again—it is a purely Roman city!

I thought:

"Maybe the legacy of ancient Carthage lives on in our bodies and minds, too, durable and indestructible, although we ourselves are not aware of it? Perhaps it is true what some strangers say that all of us—the permanent inhabitants of this land—when it comes to matters of love and hate, have in our veins not blood but fire and that we are all naturally connected to the world of sorcery?"

Our conversation soon turned to our—her son's and mine—studies in Athens at the Platonic Academy. I adored its founder and exclaimed with emphasis:

"I wish to follow as faithfully as possible in his footsteps, and that's why I'm going to Egypt. If not for my recent illness, I would have been there by now! But it now seems that I have to stay in Oea for a few more months."

Pudentilla was unfamiliar with Platonic philosophy and had not read a single dialogue of our master. However, as befits a cultured woman, she was interested in poetry and asked if Plato had left any poems. I replied that as a young man, he was a poet and even wrote dramas. However, he burned all those writings when he decided to devote himself exclusively to philosophy at a decisive moment in his life.

However, I added, some short poems and epigrams, written for various people he loved, have survived.

"Who were these people? And what were the poems?" asked Pudentilla, clearly interested.

I immediately regretted my careless words. After all, almost all of these epigrams worshiped boys! It did not seem fitting to me to recite these passionate poems to such a serious and stern matron. In any case, this one, in my opinion, was the most beautiful:

> *When I kissed Agathon, my soul jumped to my lips;*
> *And it stopped there, confused,*
> *As if it wanted to pass to the other side.*

But I quoted another, apparently more restrained, in which Plato speaks of one of his young disciples, a boy named Aster, or Star:

> *You are staring at the stars, my Star.*
> *How I would like to become the heavens*
> *To look at you with a thousand eyes!*

The boy died in his youth. The Master offered this epigram to his shadow:

> *In the past, you shone among the living as the Morning Star.*
> *Now, in death, you shine among the dead as the Evening Star.*

Luckily, at that moment, another poem came to my mind, attributed by some to Plato and fortunately addressed to a girl. I immediately repeated it aloud:

> *I'm throwing you an apple. If you love me willingly,*
> *Keep it, and in return, give me what you have most precious.*
> *And if—which may gods forbid—you think otherwise,*
> *Take the fruit all the same but consider carefully*
> *That your fresh beauty will soon pass away.*

I said it, and—I froze in terror. I had before me a woman no longer of the freshest youth! Trying to save the day, I risked a new faux pas. But it seemed to me that I had little left to lose in Pudentilla's eyes. I said:

"I know another epigram whose authorship is quite commonly attributed to the founder of the Academy, although I personally am of a different opinion. The poem is bold in content and, to some extent, contradicts the last one. It goes:

> *I have Archeanassa, hetaera from Colophon.*
> *Even today, in her wrinkles, there still dwells bitter love.*
> *Poor you, who had known her when she was young.*
> *How many tribulations have you been through!*

Maybe I imagined it, but it seemed to me briefly that Pudentilla smiled a tiny smile. She obviously understood these words as I had wished. And again, I thought that perhaps the Punic language was not the only legacy of the former masters of this land but also the passionate nature of its inhabitants, worthy of the worshipers of the goddess Tanit.[4]

We agreed that I would move into the beautiful home of Pudentilla on the following day.

THE LINEN BUNDLE

I moved to my new quarters with everything I had brought from Madauros. I carried my sacred objects wrapped carefully in a linen cloth. My slave carried the rest of my belongings. He had been my only companion on my long journey. You see, when I moved into the house of this wealthy widow, my worldly possessions were rather modest. But only a year later, I was able to emancipate three people from my

---

[4] Tanit was the chief deity of Carthage alongside her consort Baal-Hamon. In modern-day Tunisian Arabic, it is customary to invoke *Omek Tannou* ('Mother Tannou') to summon rain.

service—and all of them in one day. And that was later to cause me much trouble from envious and petty people.

As soon as I crossed the threshold of the new abode, I asked where the altar of the household deities was, and I deposited my relics there. The following day I looked into that room early in the morning: I wanted to see whether, by any chance, someone curious had not peeked into my little bundle.

But how delighted I was to discover that the room was actually—a library! Numerous papyrus scrolls lay in niches and in chests. They belonged to Pontianus, who was seriously interested in philosophy and literature. That is why he had gone to Athens, where fate brought us together in the groves of the Academy. It is regrettable that even the love of knowledge and protracted study are insufficient to form constancy of character and protect us against temptations. The example of Pontianus was to prove it especially clearly.

Returning to the subject of the library, however: I discovered in it the works of Plato; treatises by other philosophers, most of them students of Socrates or Plato; and books by many Greek historians and orators. Pontianus had acquired most of these scrolls in Greece, brought them here, and left them when he went to Rome to study law. He now kindly allowed me to use these books whenever I wished. Looking at the matter from the perspective of later events, I even suspect that he was overjoyed to do so, for in this way, he bound me even more closely to his mother's house, which suited his secret plans perfectly.

Meeting after so many years an old friend from Plato's Academy; the fact that the meeting happened while I was traveling in the footsteps of Plato on a pilgrimage to Egypt, the home of gods and secret sciences; and finding all these works of Plato here, in a remote city lost between the sea and the vastness of sandy wastes—all of this seemed to me like a sign from heaven: a sign that I should take advantage of my sojourn in Oea to complete my long-cherished project of presenting in Latin the life and works of the founder of the Academy.

I did not know at that time what final shape my work might

take, for it so happened that it became entangled with the vicissitudes of my life: events that were amusing or pathetic, and sometimes dangerous, sometimes led me away from scholarly research, and sometimes inclined me to it. But I have long since seen that there are no accidents in life. Secret powers rule everything, leading us to goals known only to themselves.

At certain moments in his life, Socrates heard voices, advice, and instructions coming from somewhere. He attributed them—certainly correctly—to his *daemon* or guardian spirit. I have too little true wisdom and purity of spirit to hear what my guardian *daemon* says. However, I believe that he guides my steps, too. If that's what my enemies mean when they call me a magician and a sorcerer, so be it. But I would rate them too highly to think them capable of formulating any profound views; they only see trifles, like that linen shawl, and even these they misunderstand.

MYSTERIES

Wrapped in a linen shawl, my sacred objects accompanied me everywhere. I received them from the priests of Demeter and Persephone at Eleusis when I was initiated there. For, while studying in Athens, I did not fail to study those rites and teachings which, from times immemorial, have enjoyed special reverence throughout Hellas. Besides, Eleusis is so close to Athens—a little more than half a day's walk—that it would be a sign of disrespect not to make a pilgrimage to the sanctuary of the two goddesses, one of whom feeds us with the fruits of the earth, while the other rules over the world of the dead.

It seemed to me all the more important to do so since Eleusinian mysteries are performed only and exclusively in that locality, while the rites in honor of other deities are performed all over the empire, wherever their priests teach them, and their worshipers gather to study. I myself received an extraordinary favor from the Egyptian goddess Isis on the seashore near Corinth; and later in Rome.

She first appeared to me at night, at moonrise, and I soon joined her temple there. Later, in Rome, I saw her husband Osiris in a dream, and I ascended to a higher level of understanding of the hidden truth.

However, with some surprise and even regret, I have to say that Plato probably had not been initiated in the Eleusinian mysteries, and he barely mentions them in his works. And yet he speaks often and with great reverence about various immortal deities, about the fate of the soul, about ancient legends and teachings, about the wisdom of both Hellenic and barbarian priests and seers. The tone in the tenth book of *The Laws* is especially beautiful and very personal. Plato rebukes doubters who deny the existence of immortal gods. Here is the text of his argument:

> These doubters do not believe the stories they heard from their mothers and nurses as children, repeated like magical spells, sometimes jokingly, sometimes seriously. They heard them also at prayers and sacrifices—and such rites are among the most touching memories of our childhood. These doubters should also remember that their parents offered prayers and supplications to the gods with the deepest possible faith in their existence and out of concern for their own good and the good of their offspring. They should also understand that all Hellenes and all barbarians do this: at various moments of life, both good and bad, at the rising and the setting of the sun or the moon, devoutly bowing down, and never for an instant doubting the existence of immortal gods.

Plato was already old when he wrote *The Laws*. Who knows whether, while writing these words, he was not thinking back to the dearest memories of his childhood, when his mother, cradling him to her breast and lulling him to sleep, told him tales of good and merciful gods. Or when on holy days, his father, surrounded by the whole family and servants at the sacrificial altar in the courtyard, solemnly lifted his hands to the sky, calling in turn on various deities and asking them for mercy for all the members of his household.

And speaking of mysteries, it has just come to my mind that in his dialogue *Phaedo,* Plato put these words into the mouth of Socrates as he prepared for his death:

> The truth is really a purification from weakness. Restraint, honesty, courage, and even common sense are also kinds of inner purity. The founders of mysteries had a good idea. They were not just talking nonsense when they suggested through an allegory that he who passes unsanctified and uninitiated into the world of the dead will remain buried in dirt, but he who arrives there after initiation and purification will dwell with the gods. But as the superiors of certain mysteries used to say: "The symbol of initiation is worn by many, but true mystics are few." And in my opinion, these mystics, that is, those blessed by god, are none other than those who love wisdom in a proper way.

These words, ostensibly from Socrates but really from Plato himself, seem important to me for two reasons. First, they show that the founder of the Academy considered the study of philosophy to be a kind of initiation, but the teachings and ceremonies of various mysteries he regarded as only vague allegories of the highest knowledge, established by enlightened men in ancient times to guide the little ones who are not yet ready to hear wisdom in its purest form.

But there is a second reason why these words are important. Because what Plato says here about mysteries refers not to Eleusis but to the Orphic doctrine.[5] In many of his works, Plato both directly or indirectly refers to the great myth around which the Orphics construct their teachings and ceremonies:

> The god Dionysus was torn apart and devoured by the Titans. Shocked by this crime, Zeus burned them with his thunderbolts, and he formed the first man from their ashes. As a result, man has

---

[5] Orphism was a set of religious beliefs and practices originating in ancient Greece and associated with literature ascribed to the mythical poet Orpheus, who descended into the underworld and returned to the land of the living. The central focus of Orphism was the suffering and death of god Dionysus at the hands of the Titans.

two conflicting elements within him. One of them comes from Dionysus and is divine and immortal, and the other comes from the Titans, who were terrestrial, bestial beings. Therefore, the human body is the prison and the grave of the pure spirit, which would be equal to the gods without it. Human life is, therefore, both a punishment and trial; for the divine element in us, it is like death, while the death of the body is the true beginning of its real life. When the soul descends into Hades, it is judged, and afterward, according to its merits or vices, it either suffers in the mire of the underworld or rejoices in happiness alongside the gods.

But the same Plato introduces in the first book of *The Republic* his own brother Adeimantus who scoffs at these notions of reward and punishment after death as too naive:

> Those who tell such stories send the virtuous to Hades to feast: they set them up on banquet sofas, wine them and dine them and crown them with laurels. Evidently, they think that the best reward for virtue on earth is—eternal drunkenness in the afterlife. And they bury the wicked and the criminals in some Hades mire or order them to carry water in sieves without ceasing.

And thus, it is not easy to find out what the actual views of Plato were—and not only in this matter. The founder of the Academy lived long and wrote much. It is possible that over the years, he changed his views on even the most fundamental matters. Sometimes, too, it's hard to understand whether he says something seriously or whether he is hiding irony under the guise of sublime and beautiful words. He probably learned this skill of subtle ambiguity from his master, Socrates, but he certainly developed it to perfection. Finally, almost all of Plato's works are in the form of dialogues: do we have the right to consider as his own statements all words which he puts into the mouths of his various speakers?

It follows from these remarks that I found myself in an embarrassing position when I began to work on Plato. I had to find some solid foundation, as it were. Or, to put it better—a guiding plot so as not to get lost in this strange, wonderful, and intricate labyrinth of thought. Who knows, perhaps Plato built this labyrinth precisely to keep his deepest and most sacred secrets from the eyes of the profane?

THE SEVENTH LETTER

I now recalled my student years, when Pontianus and I had walked among the plane and olive trees of the Academy or sat in the shade of its porticoes at the feet of wise teachers who, for almost five centuries, generation after generation, had been transmitting and interpreting Plato's thoughts as they understood them. And they do not all understand them the same way. And there, in the Academy, Master Gaius,[6] the most respected teacher of that time, often remarked that the best way to know Plato's life and views was from a certain letter of his, which is sometimes called the Seventh Letter, and which had been addressed to his Sicilian friends. So in Oea, as soon as I remembered the teachings of Gaius, I immediately set about studying this letter, which is, in fact, quite a lengthy treatise.

As I have said, Pontianus had previously sussed out my intentions very carefully, keeping in mind his own goals. Several times he pointed out to me, gently and caringly, that I was thirty years old and it was time for me to start a family; after all, he himself, though a little younger, was already thinking about it. The hook of these hints, thrown as if in passing, stuck somewhere in the back of my mind because as soon as I took the Seventh Letter in my hand, I realized how old Plato had been when he composed that letter: he must have been nearly eighty. I'd never paid attention to this until now.

But here I was: reading the words of an old man at the end of his life, looking back and wanting to pass on to posterity his own vision and his own assessment of his efforts, mistakes, and achievements.

---

[6] Gaius the Platonist was a Middle Platonist philosopher active in the early to middle 2nd century AD.

And I made the following calculation:

We were in the twelfth year of the reign of the emperor Antoninus Pius, in the 232nd Olympiad,[7] and since Plato wrote the Seventh Letter during the 107th Olympiad,[8] one hundred and twenty-five Olympiads passed since then, or around five hundred years. The fact that almost exactly five centuries were now closing seemed to me to be significant and boding well for my work.

And now for the Seventh Letter.

Plato thinks back to the years of his early youth and writes right at the beginning :

> As a young man, I experienced something that happens to many. As soon as I reached adulthood, I wanted to devote myself to politics. Meanwhile, the situation of the state looked like this:
>
> Because many had been critical of the political system of the time, there was a coup. Fifty-one citizens headed the new authorities. Of this number, eleven supervised commerce and administration in Athens itself, and ten administered Piraeus. The other thirty managed all the central state offices with unlimited powers.
>
> It so happened that some of them were my relatives and friends. They immediately began to encourage me to take part in their work, as it also concerned me. It is not surprising that I was under some delusions at the time. I was very young, after all, and naïve enough to think that these men would lead the country from its former chaos to the rule of law. So I watched carefully how the new rulers would behave. And what did I see? Behold, in a short time, they made the former regime appear golden!
>
> They wanted to send an old man dear to me, whom I would not hesitate to call the most righteous man among his contemporaries, along with a few others, to go, arrest, and fetch by force a citizen sentenced to death. Why? They wanted Socrates to become an accomplice in their affairs, even against his will. But he did not obey them. He was willing to submit to the regime but was not prepared

---

[7] AD 150
[8] 352-349 BC

to participate in its crimes.

So this was young Plato. He was not interested in mysteries, nor even in the study of philosophy, but—in politics. I admit that I find this difficult to understand. In our blissful epoch of autocracy, I am used to having someone else making all decisions in matters of the state and the community, and I applaud each and every one of them.[9]

LIBER PATER

Nor am I the only man for whom all questions of politics are dead. I can safely say that this is the attitude of the broadest masses of our empire, except, of course, for a small group of high dignitaries who actually have some influence on the course of affairs. But how many religious brotherhoods, how many initiations, how many cults of various deities are there today in all the lands of our empire!

For example, in our province, and therefore also here in Oea, there are many worshipers of Liber Pater, which is to say the Greek god Dionysus-Bacchus. His confraternities, which one can only enter by initiation, gather for strange services, consisting primarily of joint feasting. And what feasting it is! The wine pours profusely, and the cheerful mystics dance practically naked and ever more passionately to the accompaniment of rhythmic and poignant music. They dance until some of them fall into a kind of frenzy, which then spreads to all the others. They later claim that the spirit of god had entered them and that they were not in control. They scream in ecstasy, they howl, they jump, they roll on the ground, tearing apart various objects to shreds, they embrace and love each other. All this, in their opinion, is a foretaste of eternity, in which they, the faithful worshipers of Dionysus, will participate in the divine feast of the immortal gods.

I understand these ideas. How else can simple and uneducated people imagine happiness but as delights of the table and the bed? It

------

[9] As a Russian intellectual might say today.

was no different five centuries ago, in Plato's time, although the excitement of real political life made these phenomena something less prominent. But even then, the indecency of Bacchic ceremonies was condemned. Joint feasts, drunkenness, and orgies shocked the people of that time as much as they shock us today.

At least, that's what I understand from a brief reference in the second book of Plato's *Laws*. The story was spread that the stepmother of the god Dionysus, Hera, deprived him of clear discernment. In revenge, Dionysus introduced Bacchic festivals and crazy celebrations and also gave us wine. Thus, if Plato is to be believed, some of his contemporaries explained the unusual cult of Bacchus—so strikingly different from the solemnity of the ceremonies in honor of other gods—by a conflict among the immortals. However, Plato himself did not agree with this view because he commented:

> I leave the spreading of this story to those who think it safe to make pronouncements about the gods.

Plato had his own views about the origins and meaning of song, dance, and—even wine. He considered them our inheritance from the period of the infancy of humanity: a necessary inheritance because from it arose our sense of rhythm and harmony, proper among all beings, not only man, and crucial in the process of perfecting the soul and the body.

POETRY AND ITS CENSORS

Since I have mentioned upbringing, I wish at once to raise a matter concerning the views of Plato, which has puzzled me ever since I came across it.

Plato wrote his great work, *The Laws,* at the end of his life to elucidate his ideas concerning the correct principles of educating the citizens of a perfect state. This shaping of personality begins in the earliest childhood and continues until old age. Thus, in the perfect state, all citizens are subject to the constant and strict rigor of laws governing their conduct in public and private life. Only those citizens who have reached the age of sixty are free to arrange their affairs more freely, but of course, by then, by the time they have reached their old age, they are so wholly and perfectly formed that they themselves become an embodiment of the law. And thus, the old must judge the young and their adherence to the system. Even days of rest, or festivals in honor of the gods, are part of this universal education. In part, they are intended to offer relaxation and to make life more pleasant, which is why they are filled with music, dance, and choral singing. However, the form and content of these works have to comply with certain laws. Plato established and discussed them in the seventh book of *The Laws*.

The first law requires that the mood of the works should be sublime. The second, that the songs ought to be a kind of prayer addressed to the gods and that poets must make sure that nothing wicked slips into their works, which might provoke the wrath of the immortals. But since it is well known that artists often do not know what is good and what is bad, the third law says: the artist must not deviate from what the state considers to be right, beautiful, and good. He is not even allowed to show his work to private persons until judges and censors have approved it. The subject of the songs are to be primarily gods but may also be demons, heroes, and even dead people, as long as they were once meritorious to the state. On the other hand, praising living people, even eminent ones, required caution.

But what to do with the works bequeathed to us by past generations? The answer is that the old men must pick and choose among them, rejecting anything that is wrong. And what is of some value should be handed over to talented poets and musicians so that they can make appropriate alterations. It is necessary to use the talents of the creators, but in such a way as to leave as little room as possible for their personal opinions. Ultimately, everything is to be decided by the will of the guardians of the system. A piece expressing the correct content is a thousand times better than a disorderly piece, even if the former lacks the seductive charm of the sweet Muse.

Such were the views of Plato, the old man. The same Plato who, in his youth and even in his middle age, wrote passionate love elegies. I had them fresh in my memory due to the recent conversation with Pudentilla. Perhaps that is why the matter seemed to me even more puzzling than usual and the contradiction of the two attitudes astonishingly glaring.

For a moment, I thought that everything was basically simple and clear: towards the end of his life, the philosopher became—as old people usually do—tough, uncompromising, impervious to the charms of youthful experiences, and perhaps even opposed to them out of old-age envy. But then I realized that Plato had already expressed similar views in a work he wrote in his prime. I am thinking of the tenth book of his *Republic*.

CONCERNING THE HARM OF POETRY

The interlocutors in that book are Socrates and Glaucon, Plato's brother. I guess this is meaningful: perhaps by putting his thoughts in the mouths of his closest associates, the philosopher wanted to indicate that they were not a game or a joke, but his own, profoundly held views.

Right at the beginning, Socrates puts forward a thesis that has already appeared in the dialogue before, but has not yet been fully developed:

> "We will never be perfect in our country if we tolerate imitative poetry!"

The definition of imitative poetry is very broad and covers virtually all types of poetry (except for two, which are discussed below) because epics, and drama, and lyric poetry all try, each in its own way, to imitate reality and to arouse in the listeners the emotions that real events would cause in them. Socrates attacks poetry somewhat in spite of himself. He confesses that he loved and worshiped Homer from childhood—Homer, the forefather of this kind of poetry—but criticizes him sharply, both him and his followers—as well as the tragedians and the lyricists, who in their works give a semblance or illusion of reality.

It is in vain to ask, argues Socrates, which state has improved its laws and constitution, won a war, or introduced some technical innovation thanks to Homer. Besides, Homer was neither a teacher nor a model, even for his contemporaries or those closest to him, and he never established a "Homeric way of life," as Pythagoras, for example, did.

But according to Socrates, the most serious objection to imitative poetry concerns its very nature:

Imitative poetry stimulates and excites the emotional element of the soul at the expense of the rational. This is both harmful and dangerous. It is as if in a state, someone gave power to the stupid and let them rule but inhibited or even destroyed the rational and the wise. And this is exactly what the poet does: he instills in the souls of his listeners an evil system, favoring the irrational factors. This brings harm even to thinking people. Consider a relatively simple example: it often happens that Homer, or some playwright, introduces a suffering, despairing hero. We read and listen with emotion, we allow ourselves to be moved, and we praise the poet as a great artist. And yet, if the same blow falls upon ourselves, we try to remain calm and bear our misfortune with fortitude, rightly thinking that it befits a man to control his emotions. Similar harm happens when the poet excites our erotic lust, anger, or, indeed, any passion at all. In fact, such emotions should be tamed if we want to become both better and happier.

And so, the final conclusion of the two interlocutors is this: In a perfect state, we will only allow—as far as poetry is concerned—hymns to the gods and hymns in praise of honest men. For as soon as the sweet Muse of lyrical song and epic appears, she will subvert the rule of law and reason and let loose the unbridled pursuit of emotional sensations.

Bosschère

Such were the views of Plato according to the tenth book of his *Republic*.

When I read this dialogue, as well as *The Laws*, a suspicion arises in me that the Academy presented to us a very single-sided image of its founder. Our teachers always spoke of him as a sage lost in lofty thought on the topics of Truth, Beauty, and Goodness, living entirely in a world of pure, otherworldly ideas. And yet, as I read these dialogues, I find it hard to resist the thought that this man was obsessed with... politics and lust for power. He wanted to change everything, transform everything. He had no regard for the voice of tradition. He even trampled on his own loves like Homer. He wanted to create a new state, a new system, a new man. Yes, yes, it was all ostensibly in order to realize the unity of beauty and truth and goodness in an ideal state. But at what price!

If so, I thought, Plato must have experienced in his youth shocks that alienated him from his homeland and set him against all political systems with which he came into contact.

Now, I began this study of Plato's life with the Seventh Letter. I read in it that in his youth, he had been interested in politics and had wanted to devote himself to it but became disgusted and discouraged by the conduct of the Athenian government of the time, even though his relatives were in office. And the worst of all the wrongdoings of that government was that it tried to implicate in its crimes his beloved teacher Socrates.

And so, I came to the conclusion that I had to turn to that matter and study it more closely.

SOCRATES AND THE GOVERNMENT OF THIRTY

The first work of Plato I ever read—still in my childhood—was not the Seventh Letter, of course, but *The Apology of Socrates*. I believe that this work—the speech of Socrates before the Athenian court—will always remain in the program of every educational system for as long as our world can resist barbarism. I think I remember that speech by heart.

If only I could have foreseen it when picking up *The Apology* in Oea again, how soon I would have to stand trial myself and pronounce my own defense! And yet, my own case is quite similar to that of Socrates and equally dangerous: he was accused of introducing new gods and corrupting the youth, while I am accused of practicing black magic and of seducing a woman by its methods.

But do not let me anticipate events and let me return to the issue of *The Apology of Socrates*. It occurred to me that in *The Apology,* Socrates tells us in some detail how bravely he behaved when the Thirty ruled:

> They summoned me along with four other citizens. They ordered us to arrest and bring in a certain Leo from the island of Salamis. He was to be executed. Many citizens received similar orders at that time: the government did this in order to implicate as many citizens as it could in its crimes. In response, I showed—by deed not word—that I cared nothing for my own life but that I cared very much not to commit any impious or unlawful act. Not even that government, almighty as it was, could have compelled me. Not even by the threat of terror. We five left the building. The other four went to Salamis and indeed arrested and brought Leo in. Meanwhile, I went home. I would probably have paid for this insubordination with my life had I not been so fortunate that the Thirty were soon overthrown.

Plato was in his twenties when democracy was overthrown in Athens. It happened in the first year of the 94th Olympiad [404 BC] as a result of the defeat of Athens in the war with Sparta.[10] The victorious Lacedaemonians demanded that henceforth only the wealthiest citizens (numbering about three thousand) should vote in the Athenian assembly, but in fact, the Commission of Thirty was made all-powerful. The Lacedaemonians correctly reasoned that such a system would best guarantee the loyalty of the vanquished. But in Athens itself, the democrats were blamed—and not without reason— for having caused the catastrophe of the war. They were accused of having overtaxed the resources of the state; alienated her allies by brutality; and exiled or murdered many distinguished citizens because of morbid suspicions.

But, as Plato rightly says in the Seventh Letter, the ruthlessness of the new government soon made the old chaotic democracy seem golden. Within a few months, more than 1,500 death sentences were carried out in Athens, and more than 5,000 citizens were forced to flee abroad. And the Commission came to be commonly called the Tyranny of Thirty.

I was interested in what life was like in Athens when the city was under the Commission's terror, what people were persecuted, and why. It was, after all, the period when Plato was entering adulthood and wanted to enter political life, and he was, as he himself confesses, related to many of the Thirty by kinship and acquaintance.

So, I reached for the text of a man who witnessed the events and lived through many of them. I'm thinking of Lysias. Like everyone who has studied Greek rhetoric, I had to memorize his court speeches, and already then, I was struck by the story of his family under the regime of the Thirty. And now, when I reread it, it seemed to me that I was involved in those events myself—the report felt so vivid and immediate.

---

[10] The Peloponnesian War (431–404 BC)

THE STORY OF LYSIAS

My father, Cephalus, came to Athens [from Syracuse] at the invitation of Pericles. He settled here over thirty years ago. During this entire time, neither he nor any of us, his sons, has ever sued anyone or has ever had to defend himself in court. This is how we lived under democracy: we committed no offenses, and no one offended against us. But then came the rule of the Thirty, all of them criminals and perverse men. They declared that the state must be purged of vice in order that the vast masses of honest citizens might live in peace and order. However, the actions of the Thirty did not quite match their words, as my story will show..

Two members of the Commission, Theognis and Peison, put forward the following proposal during one of its meetings:

"Some foreigners living in Athens (*metoicos*) are hostile to the present regime. We should take advantage of this. We will punish some of these *metoicos* for political crimes and confiscate their property. The country is in poverty, and the government needs cash."

They easily convinced the rest because for them issuing death sentences was nothing but money was everything. The committee soon decided that ten *metoicos* would be arrested, but for the sake of appearances, two poor men would be included in their number. In this way, they thought, it would look like they took the action not to seize property but to protect the state from the enemies of the people.

Divided into working groups, they immediately set to work. When they entered my house, I was hosting guests. They chased them away and handed me over to Peison. Meanwhile, others went to our workshop to list our assets. Taking the opportunity, I asked Peison if he could save me—for a fee, of course. He agreed on the condition that the sum was worth the risk. I promised to give him a talent of silver. He accepted.

Of course, I knew perfectly well that this man had no regard for gods and men and I felt that in this situation, it was absolutely necessary to obtain from him some assurance that he would keep his word. So, I made him swear an oath:

"Let ruin come upon me and my children if I do not save Lysias when I take a talent of silver from him!"

I then entered my bedroom and opened the strongbox. Peison slipped in behind me. As soon as he saw the contents of the box, he shouted to summon his men; he ordered them to seize all the contents of the chest. There was more there than I had promised him: three talents of silver, four hundred Kizykene[11] drachmas, and four silver cups. I begged him to give me something from this wealth for my journey. And he angrily replied:

"Be content that I save your life!"

As I left the house with Peison, we came upon two other members of the Commission of Thirty who had just left my workshop. They asked where we were going. Peison replied that we were going to the house of my brother, Polemarchus, to see how things stood there. They said that he should go alone; but that I was to go with them to the house of Damnipus. Before leaving, Peison whispered to me to keep silent and be of good hope because he would be back soon and would surely defend me.

We found Theognis at Damnipus' house, watching over the rest of the prisoners. They handed me to him and left. I understood that this was my last living moment: I had to run, or else I was a dead man. I summoned Damnipus and said to him:

"You are my kith, I am now in your house. I've never done you any harm, and they're going to kill me because I'm rich. Save me."

He promised he would. But he thought it best to tell Theognis, who (he whispered to me) would do anything for money. So, he went into another room to talk to Theognis.

I knew the house well and knew that it had two entrances. I felt I had to try to escape. I reasoned: if I slip through, I will survive; and if they capture me, they'll let me go anyway, as long as Damnipus

---

[11] Coins struck by the city of Cyzicus

persuades Theognis.

And so I ran away. There were three doors through which I had to pass, and they were all unlocked and my jailors were only guarding the main gate! I sought refuge in the house of an acquaintance who owned a ship. I sent him to the city to find out about my brother Polemarchus. He soon returned, but with bad news: Polemarchus had been apprehended in the street and imprisoned. That same night, I sailed to Megara. Meanwhile, the Commission of Thirty passed their usual sentence on Polemarchus: they ordered him to drink hemlock. And that without even giving him a reason why he should die, let alone a court hearing or the possibility of self-defense.

Polemarchus's corpse was released from prison. We owned three houses, but the Commission did not allow the body to be taken to any of them, and we had to rent some shack to hold the wake and take him to his grave from there. Most of our garments had been confiscated, and when the family asked for a robe to cover the corpse, they did not receive a scrap. One of my friends donated a *himation*,[12] another a head support. Everyone gave what they could so that somehow the funeral could take place.

The Commission of Thirty seized from us seven hundred shields. They took so much silver, gold, and bronze, ornaments, and women's dresses that, I imagine, none of its members had ever dreamed of such riches. But this was not enough for the tyrants. In their greed, they went so far that one of them removed with his own hands a set of gold earrings from the ears of Polemarchus's wife.

PLATO AND THE FAMILY OF LYSIAS

Such business went on in Athens when Plato entered his adult life. It's hard to believe it, especially for me, who know the Athens of today: a calm, quiet town of monuments and arts, as if immersed in meditation

---

[12] *Himation*: an outer garment worn by the ancient Greeks over the left shoulder and under the right arm.

on its past greatness. A town of philosophers, making a living mainly thanks to its students and tourists. If there is ever an argument in Athens today, it is usually between different schools of philosophers. And how ancient is the saying: sooner two clocks will reconcile than two philosophers!

And how many philosophers there are in Athens! The Academy, the immortal creation of Plato is flourishing The Lyceum, founded by Aristotle, thrives. The Stoa, the brainchild of Zeno, is still alive. The garden of Epicure still blooms in flower. There are also the coarse cynics, distant descendants of Diogenes, as well as the subtle and humble skeptics.

Yes, there are also disagreements among its citizens, especially during elections to the municipal council. For the old offices with their beautiful names still survive, and some people are still flattered to hold them. However, these ambitions are small and almost ridiculous, for all these Athenian dignities are only a pretense and a fiction since no real political power attaches to them. Centuries ago, of course, it was different. Back then, there was a real struggle for power, for property, for freedom.

As I read the account of Lysias, I reflect, with joy and contentment, how blessed I am to live in my times. I don't have to deal with politics. The reins of government are in the hands of people appointed by the will of the gods. Throughout the length and breadth of our Empire, peace and law reign. Therefore, instead of occupying ourselves with trivial matters of state, we can devote all our energy to what is really important, great, and eternal: the mysteries of being and of the heavens.

That's what I thought at the time, anyway—naïve me. I had no clue that, in our happy times, my sincere and complete devotion to scientific research could bring down utter misery upon me; threaten my reputation, my fortune, and even my life.

However, that was yet to happen. For the time being, I was only interested in the Athens of five hundred years ago and blissfully unaware of my future. I lived the tragedy of Lysias' family. His brother Polemarchus was seized in the street and put to death without trial; all his property was confiscated; and Lysias only saved himself by fleeing at the last moment but had to go into exile. The unfortunate fate of this family must have made a great impression on Plato if only because he knew all its members very well since boyhood. Indeed, Polemarchus and Lysias were already adults when he met them for the first time. But while they and their father, Cephalus, remained in his memory as venerable seniors, Plato's elder brothers socialized with the two sons; they moved in the same circles, they had mutual friends, and above all, they all shared an attachment to Socrates.

There was, however, a fundamental difference between the families of Plato and Lysias. The former were native Athenians from times immemorial and were even considered aristocratic; the latter were *metoicos*, that is to say, resident aliens, and they had no civic privileges. Lysias himself confirms this.

Cephalus had come to Athens at the invitation of Pericles. He and his sons made many contributions to the state, but they did not have full political rights. Despite this, they felt attached to their chosen homeland, where, thanks to their armorers' workshop, they gained considerable wealth. These riches aroused much envy and were later to be the cause of the ruin of the house, but they allowed Polemarchus and Lysias to associate with the local aristocracy on an equal footing.

About their faithful service, Lysias wrote with pride:

We covered all the costs of the training of the choir. We did whatever we were told. We paid many extraordinary taxes. We always did the right thing. We had no enemies. We ransomed many Athenians from slavery. As *metoicos*, we were more useful to the state than the Commission of Thirty as a government.

Plato did not like Lysias, but he paid a beautiful and eloquent homage to the memory of Polemarchus and Cephalus. And he chose his house in Piraeus for the setting of his great dialogue, a dialogue which he probably began to write some thirty years after the death of Polemarchus. I am thinking of *The Republic,* of course, because I recognize the profound wisdom of this treatise, although other works of the divine philosopher are closer to my heart. The opening passages of *The Republic* are captivating because of their simplicity and vividness. They describe the way in which the meetings of Socrates and his friends, their conversations and discussions, took place: accidentally and simply.

As for those of you who do not know or who may have forgotten, I must remind you that this conversation about the constitution of the ideal republic is supposed to have taken place five years before the end of the Peloponnesian War. Plato was too young to attend; he must have heard about the great disputation from his brothers, Glaucon and Adeimantus. He gave them prominent roles in his tale. Here is how it begins:

A MEETING IN PIREUS

I went to Piraeus yesterday with Glaucon, Ariston's son. I wanted to pray to the goddess and take the opportunity to watch the ceremonies in her honor. I was curious how they would turn out because they were being held for the first time. Well, the procession of the residents seemed beautiful to me, but the procession of the Thracians looked just as good. And after we had prayed and seen our fill, we set off for Athens. But Polemarchus, son of Cephalus, spotted us from afar. He sent his boy after us to hold us until he caught up. The boy grabbed me by the *himation* and said:

"Polemarchus asks you to wait!"

I turned around and asked:

"Where is he?"

And the boy:

"He's just behind me. Wait!"

"All right, we'll wait," Glaucon and I agreed.

Immediately Polemarchus arrived and with him, Adeimantus, brother of Glaucon, and Nikeratus, son of Nikias, and many others returning from the procession. Polemarchus asked:

"It seems to me, Socrates, that you're heading back to the city?"

"And you're not mistaken," I replied.

"And do you see how many of us are here?"

"Certainly."

"Well, then, you must either wrestle us all or stay to dinner."

"Is there no other option? Could we not reason about it?"

"Can you convince men who will not listen?"

"Certainly not!" interjected Glaucon.

"Then be informed that we will not listen!"

And Adeimantus added:

"I guess you don't know that there will be a horse race with torches in the evening in honor of the goddess?"

I shouted:

"A horserace! Something completely new! Will they pass torches from hand to hand while racing on horseback? I guess that's what you're talking about?"

"Exactly!" Polemarchus exclaimed. "And besides, they're going to have a midnight service, a very interesting thing in itself. We'll sup then go to see it. And surely we'll meet lots of young people there, and we'll talk. So, stay with us, won't you?"

THE GODDESS BENDIS

I should now interrupt my story briefly in order to explain a few things. First of all, perhaps you would like to know who this unnamed goddess was, in whose honor celebrations were held in Piraeus. Plato does not tell us her name, but it is easy to guess: the goddess was Bendis, an important deity of the Thracians.[13] Piraeus, the port city of Athens, had long been home to a large colony of Thracian merchants

---

[13] Thrace lay where today's Bulgaria lies.

and sailors, and they brought their goddess with them.

And she remains there today. Believers see her as the mistress of mountains, forests, and animals, so the Hellenes often identify her with Artemis. However, she must also be a giver of fertility since she receives from Thracian women an offering of ears of wheat. I attended the services in honor of Bendis when I studied in Athens, for I always try to learn about foreign religious cults. After all, each has its peculiar mysteries, each contains a grain of truth, and every grain of truth is helpful.

The Thracian rites, I must admit, are very impressive: they are accompanied by the sounds of very loud, rhythmic music of pipes, drums, and tympanums, and the dances are almost orgiastic in nature. They attract crowds of tourists, and they did five centuries ago.

The Athenians inducted Bendis into their pantheon in the last years of the Peloponnesian War. I once read an inscription commemorating this fact on one of the tablets on the Acropolis. It said that in addition to the processions, which had long been staged by the Thracian colony, there would now also be a procession of Athenians in Piraeus. The holiday—now as centuries ago—falls on June 7 and lasts all night. And therefore, it was on this day that Socrates went to Piraeus to pay homage to the goddess, for he was a man of great piety, and to see the procession by Athenians, then held for the first time.

Naturally, I, too, traveled from Athens to Piraeus on June 7 for the same purpose. A dozen of us walked from the Academy. Pontianus walked with me. We treated this trek—two hours along a fairly busy commercial road—like a pilgrimage for, at every step of the way, we remembered that on the same day, five centuries earlier, Socrates had walked over the same flagstones to worship the same goddess, just like us.

It is easy to imagine that, five hundred years earlier, the news of the new feast brought to Piraeus not only crowds of pious people but also swarms of boys. They were mostly interested in the horse race, of course, with its passing of torches from hand to hand and all. What a spectacle! Athens at that time did not have circus games, which in our era are organized on every occasion, even in small towns. It is no wonder then that the horserace was an extraordinary attraction.

I imagine that what happened was this:

We know that Plato was interested in all sorts of games and competitions and that in his youth, he was a good wrestler, so he was probably among the boys who'd gone to see the race. Older brothers were supposed to watch over the younger ones. Glaucon went, accompanied by Socrates, and the other brother, Adeimantus, went with Polemarchus, and the two groups met in the evening on the road leading to Athens. So the boy probably witnessed the humorous dispute: whether to yield to Polemarchus's pleas and stay in his house in Piraeus or to return to Athens. He remembered this conversation well and reconstructed it vividly years later.

As it happened, they all went to Polemarchus's house. There were quite a few guests there, including the head of the family, old Cephalus. Little Plato was probably placed in one of the side rooms and told to wait until they all went to watch the Thracian horse race. Meanwhile, the elders entertained themselves with conversation. Years later, Plato presented it according to what his inspiration dictated.

I would like to recall the discussion between Socrates and Cephalus because it has a bearing on our topic, it is important, even though it is quite natural and playful, and it will allow me to discuss my own trials and tribulations.

So, I let Socrates speak:

THE BENEFITS OF OLD AGE

Cephalus seemed to me to have advanced in age, perhaps because I hadn't seen him for a long time. Crowned with a wreath, he was resting on a chaise with a support under his head. He had just finished the evening sacrifice in the courtyard. We sat next to him on sofas arranged in a semicircle.

The old man greeted us, and he spoke to me in a tone of light reprimand:

"My Socrates, you don't visit us enough in Piraeus! And it behooves you to visit us, for if it were easier for me to travel to the city, we would be visiting you all the time. You must know that while all my bodily pleasures are dying away, good conversations still give me lively pleasure, and I long for them. So I beg you: do not neglect your acquaintance with these young people but do come to me because we are friends."

I replied:

"Actually, I enjoy talking to men advanced in years. I think that it is worth asking their views since they have already traveled a road that still lies before me, whether steep and hard or easy and comfortable. I would especially like to know from you who are upon what the poets call the threshold of old age, how this end of life seems to you: is it difficult or otherwise?"

Cephalus replied:

"Very well, I will tell you how I see it. I meet quite often a group of my peers. Most lament, regretting the lost pleasures of youth. They remember the joys of love, wine, games, and all that sort of thing. They grieve as if something wonderful had been taken away from them, as if they had lived wonderfully then but now barely vegetated. Some complain about being treated badly by the household. They lament over their age and how many misfortunes it brings. But it seems to me that they complain about the wrong things. Because if their misfortunes were due to old age, I would suffer them, too. Meanwhile, I don't, and I know others who do not. I was once in the company of the poet Sophocles when someone asked him if he could still love a woman. And he said:

"'Oh, be still, young man! I am relieved to be rid of that thing and feel as if I have been liberated from the clutches of a cruel madman.'

"I thought that he spoke well. I thought so then, and I think so now. Because in old age, you really get complete peace and freedom from all these temptations and desires. And when they quiet down, what Sophocles described comes about: liberation from a whole host of raging despots. And here is the main source of all the troubles and complaints of old people: it is not the age, but their disposition. For those who are of good and gentle nature feel old age to be endurable. For others, however, it is as hard as youth."

I was delighted by the words of Cephalus, and I wanted to hear more from him, so I asked:

"I don't think many people would agree with your views. They would say that you easily tolerate your old age not because of your disposition but because of your wealth. There is even this proverb: a rich man has many consolations."

"You speak the truth, Socrates, for indeed, many disagree with me. And they are partly right, but not as much as they think. For Themistocles once spoke well when the inhabitant of the islet of Serifos reproached him, saying:

"'You owe your fame not to yourself but to the power of your homeland!'

To which Themistocles replied:

"'I think you are partly right. For neither would I be famous, had been born on Serifos, nor you, if you had been born in Athens.'

"In the same way, a well-disposed person does not easily endure old age if he is poor. On the other hand, someone who is difficult to live with will not be able to stand it, even if he is wealthy."

I dared to probe further:

"And how is it with you, Cephalus? Is your wealth largely inherited, or did you acquire it yourself?

Cephalus replied honestly:

"What have I acquired? As a businessman, I'm something between my grandfather and my father. For my grandfather, who bore the same name as me, inherited about as much wealth as I have now and then enlarged it many times. But my father, Lysanias, made our fortune much smaller than it is now. And now I am happy to leave it to my sons a fortune that is not smaller but not much larger than the one I inherited."

I then revealed to him the reason for my questions:

"I asked you about this because it seems to me that you are not too attached to money. This is often a trait of people who did not have to make their own fortune. On the other hand, those who have acquired riches by their own efforts love them twice over: as poets do their works, or as fathers love their children, and as all do, for their usefulness. So I don't like their company very much because they care too much about money."

PONTIANUS REVEALS HIS HAND

From the moment of my arrival in Oea, this conversation between Socrates and Cephalus, as reported by Plato in the first book of *The Republic*, took on a special meaning for me. It remained with me because: first, I reread the book at the house of Pudentilla while collecting materials for my biography of Plato, and, second, because soon afterward, I had to resort to some of its ideas in self-defense. It happened like this:

I was beginning to regain my strength and soon recovered enough to relent to my friend's requests that I give a public keynote address. The fame of my learning and oratorical talents must have grown considerably, for a huge crowd packed the basilica where the meeting was arranged. And when I had finished speaking, the audience chanted in unison over and over again:

"Excellent! Excellent!"

The most eminent personalities of the city demanded long and insistently that I should settle down among them and take the citizenship of Oea. And when the crowd had dispersed at last, Pontianus came over to congratulate me. We were returning home, just the two of us, on foot, without servants. Taking advantage of the opportunity—(as I later judged) of the gathering darkness and my joy at my recent public triumph, my friend decided to launch his assault. He started from general principles that I should regard this unanimous acceptance of the community as a good omen, a sign sent by the gods, and that I should establish my home there and start a family, taking advantage of the welcome and admiration of his fellow citizens. After this lengthy introduction, he finally blurted out what he really meant:

"If you don't mind, I'd like to help you with a suggestion. Why should you not marry my mother? You must know that many here would very much like to take her into their home. But I would only trust you for that role because you have been like a brother to me since our time at the Academy. Admittedly, I am not setting you up with a pretty girl but with a mother of children and a woman of average looks. So maybe you don't want to accept this burden. Perhaps you'd rather wait a bit longer and look around for a better match. But remember that by refusing my request, you will be acting neither like a friend nor like a philosopher!"

It is easy to understand that upon hearing these words, I stopped dead in my tracks. Nothing of the sort had ever occurred to me. But beyond the unexpected nature of this matrimonial proposal, it amazed me in its form: a strange mix of sincerity and cold calculation and—its final appeal to the lofty duties of a friend and a philosopher. I now saw in a different light the kind invitation to stay at Pudentilla's house to enjoy the view of the sea!

So I remained stunned and silent while he seemed to breathe a sigh of relief after getting the matter off his chest. He took me by the arm and began, most calmly, to describe his mother's affairs, not sparing some rather intimate details.

THE STORY OF PUDENTILLA

And here is what he told me:

My father, Sicinus, died fourteen years ago. He orphaned Pudens and me. Pudens was only a year old at the time, and I was still a long way from adulthood, so our grandfather, the father of Sicinus, was our legal guardian. Our mother, a worthy woman, devoted herself exclusively to the housekeeping and raising of her children. However, she made no secret of her intention to remarry. After all, she was a young woman at the time of Sicinus' death, twenty-something, quite handsome, and very wealthy. Because you must know that her fortune is now far greater than what our father left us.

No wonder that a whole host of suitors soon appeared. All these were people from the best houses, not only of our city but of the whole province. However, my grandfather was watching. He wanted her fortune to remain in our family, and it is hard to hold that against him. So he chased the suitors out of the house. And since this was not enough (for my mother was weary of her prolonged widowhood), he announced that he himself would choose her a husband. He had two other sons, Clarus and Emilianus. And he demanded that she marry the former. She flatly refused. First, because he was an old man and, second, because, I must say this though he is my uncle, he is a simpleton without any refinements. But my grandfather threatened that if she did not marry Clarus, he would not leave us a penny of his fortune. And he knew well that my mother loved us above all else and that she would rather give up her own happiness than let her sons suffer a financial loss.

He guessed right. Pudentilla relented, but she had handled the whole thing very prudently. She knew that our grandfather would not last long because he was old and sick. So she agreed to a marriage contract with Clarus. The contract was drawn up, but she kept postponing the wedding under various pretexts. I can't tell you what reasons she gave because I was away in Athens, but whatever they were, the wedding never took place, my grandfather died, and we, his grandchildren, were listed as the main heirs in his will, with the proviso that I, already an adult, should have custody of Pudens. It was then that I interrupted my studies at the Academy and returned to Oea to embrace my legacy. After completing the legal formalities, I left immediately, this time for Rome.

Suitors began to visit our house again, even though my mother had advanced in years somewhat. This time she decided to get married, and she had excellent reasons: she began to suffer from some unpleasant female ailments, and the doctors and midwives all agreed that the cause of the disease was the lack of proper conjugal life. They also advised me to save Pudentilla's health—and perhaps life—while her age still allowed it. My other uncle Emilianus wrote to me about this in Rome, directly and without obfuscation: 'I know that she wants to and should get married, but I don't know whom she will choose.' My mother also informed me about everything: she did not even hide the cause of her ailments.

Nor can I deny the soundness of her reasoning. She says that she won for us, her sons, our grandfather's legacy at the price of her own happiness and health; that by managing well, she increased our fortune; that I am already grown up and could marry myself, and Pudens will soon put on a man's robe. And therefore, it is high time for her to say goodbye to loneliness and to remedy her chronic illness. She also constantly assures us that she will love us as much in marriage as she does now; and that we should not fear that she might harm her children in her will.

After receiving my uncle's and mother's letters, I immediately left Rome for Oea. I was afraid lest she marry some gold digger, for such a man would surely steal all our property. This happens often. All hope for a better future, mine and my brother's, is based on our fortune. My grandfather hadn't really left us much behind. The mother's fortune, on the other hand, is estimated at some four million sesterces. Part of this is due to us as an inheritance from our father, but we have no evidence for this. Our mother, as usually happens in the family, managed everything together. But after her marriage, all of that could be lost, and if there were a legal fight, the process could be long and very costly. You understand that at present, I cannot demand my share from her because she will think that I do not trust her and would hurt me in her will. So I live in fear and see no way out. Or rather, I didn't see it until recently. Fortunately, you came to Oea, sent us by the gods. You're quite wealthy, so you won't care about our mother's money. Besides, I am well aware of your nobility and devotion to scholarship alone. So all our hope lies in you!

It would take too long to repeat all my arguments with which I tried to convince Pontianus that I could not grant his request. I presented them on our way home and in the following days because my friend continued to insist. I referred, of course, to my intended trip to Alexandria and to the study of philosophy, which consumes all my time and energy. Bearing in mind the recently read conversation between Cephalus and Socrates, I also quoted Sophocles's statement mentioned there: that he relinquished the affairs of love with the greatest delight as if he had escaped from the clutches of a madman. I confessed that I, though only thirty years old, also wanted to free myself and become utterly indifferent to all temptations of Aphrodite.

To which Pontianus replied:

"Exactly! That's the whole point! I am not recommending a sweet doll to you but a mature woman. She will not distract you too much from your study and meditation. You must marry one day anyhow because it is the right thing to do, and as a philosopher, you will not find a better opportunity."

And so we argued back and forth for many days.

THE FORTUNE OF PLATO

In the natural course of things, our constant conversations about the financial affairs of the Pontianus family made me wonder what the financial position of those great men of five centuries ago had been, men who were daily in my thoughts as I read and wrote. Besides, considerations of this kind gave me a kind of consolation: that even then, in such distant antiquity, money was already very important, and family connections mattered a lot, even among philosophers.

Cephalus stated to Socrates that he had not acquired much wealth. However, it turned out that, on the contrary, he owned too much. If it had not been for his family's wealth, the Thirty Tyrants would not have moved to seize it; Polemarchus would not have died, and Lysias would not have had to flee. So Cephalus left his sons a great inheritance but a sinister one. Fortunately for him, the old man did not live to see those tragic events.

As for Socrates, the matter is well known. He owned almost nothing. And in adulthood, he even gave up his occupation—not a bad source of living, actually—which he had inherited from his father: he was a stone mason. He lived, I believe, hand-to-mouth and chiefly by the grace of his powerful friends. He left the care of the house and children entirely to his wife, Xanthippe. He himself spent most of his time in gymnasiums and in the agora; and he often visited his acquaintances, as he did on that evening when he visited Cephalus and Polemarchus in Piraeus.

Adeimantus and Glaucon were, as I said, Plato's elder brothers. Their father was Ariston, and their mother, Perictione. This family was certainly wealthy, but today it is difficult to determine what wealth it had. In fact, all that can be said about it comes down to us in Plato's will. It reads:

These things have been left and disposed of by Plato:

An estate in Iphistiadae, bounded on the north by the road from the temple at Cephisia, on the south by the temple of Heracles in Iphistiadae, on the east by the property of Archestratus of Phrearrhi, on the west by that of Philippus of Chollidae. This it shall be unlawful for anyone to sell or alienate, but it shall be the property of the boy Adeimantus for all intents and purposes.

The estate in Eiresidae, which I bought of Callimachus, bounded on the north by the property of Eurymedon of Myrrhinus, on the south by the property of Demostratus of Xypete, on the east by that of Eurymedon of Myrrhinus, and on the west by the Cephisus.

Three minae of silver; a silver vessel weighing 165 drachmas; a cup weighing 45 drachmas; a gold signet-ring and earring weighing together four drachmas and three obols. Euclides, the stone mason, owes me three minae.

I enfranchise Artemis.

I leave four household servants, Tychon, Bictas, Apollonides, and Dionysius.

Household furniture, as set down in the inventory of which Demetrius has the duplicate.

I owe no debt.

My executors are Leosthenes, Speusippus, Demetrius, Hegias, Eurymedon, Callimachus, and Thrasippus.

I quoted this testament to prove that even a great mind, one practically divine, one looking directly at universal ideas that are crystal clear and eternal, can and should take care of its earthly affairs scrupulously and make inventories of everything he leaves behind in accordance with the formal requirements of the law.

Its first point indicates that Plato's ancestral property, inherited from his father and his forefathers, was located in Iphistiadai, i.e., in the fertile valley of the River Cephisus, in the heart of Attica. In passing it on to his brother's grandson, the young Adeimantus, Plato stipulates that this land must not be disposed of in any way. It was the Athenian principle that the ancestral estate should always remain in the same family, passing from generation to generation.

Also, it seems that Plato farmed well and prudently since he was able to afford to buy another estate, also on Cephisus, as well as land near Athens, in the grove of Academos, where he founded his school. He did not mention the Academy in his will because it no longer belonged to him. And—note!—Plato had no debts! He speaks of this with pride: "I owe no debt."

And since my spiritual master acted so prudently in the matter of property, this thought came to my mind:

I have inherited something from my father in Madauros, yes, but why should I not acquire some other fortune, perhaps in Oea, for instance? Especially since I don't have to work for it! On the contrary, money practically pushes itself into my hands. Of course, it's not all about Pudentilla's fortune, all those millions. Her dowry alone would suffice.

Bosschère

ARISTON AND PERICTIONE

I know Attica well. It is a small peninsula, not very fertile, half covered with rocky hills. Only the valley of Cephisus and the plain near Eleusis are fertile, and only there can you find more significant rural estates. But even the largest farms of Attica are ridiculously small compared to the huge *latifundia*[14] in our province of Africa. Thus even five centuries ago, in the time of Plato, landed wealth, however large, could not have been the basis of true wealth; for it did not generate income comparable to that of bold merchant ventures or craftsmen's workshops—such as, for example, the armorer's workshop of Cephalus and his sons. So the pride of Plato's family lay not so much in wealth as in their ancient, pure Attic origin.

Ariston is said to have counted among his ancestors those ancient kings who had ruled Athens a millennium ago, and through them, he traced his lineage to Poseidon, the god of the sea. But it does not seem to me that Ariston's ancestors were in any way illustrious; at most, they have perhaps held a higher office or another, for nowhere in the works of Plato do we find any mention of the relatives or ancestors of his father. Whereas he mentions various people on his mother's side frequently, and some even appear as characters in his dialogues. Apparently, then, the maternal branch of the family was closer to Plato's heart—or, at any rate, more familiar to him. Perhaps we can explain this by the fact that Ariston died when Plato was still a boy.

The mother of Adeimantus, Glaucon, Plato, and their sisters was Perictione. She came from a great family, which had given Athens several archons—the highest officials of the state. But his greatest pride was his kinship with Solon, the famous lawgiver of almost two centuries earlier and one of the founders of Athenian democracy. Plato mentions Solon many times, which proves that the tradition of family

---

[14] A *latifundium* is a very extensive parcel of privately owned land. *Latifundia* of Roman history were great landed estates specializing in agriculture destined for export: grain, olive oil, or wine.

ties with this eminent politician and poet was very much alive in Perictione's house.

After Ariston's death, Perictione married Pyrilampes, a very handsome and wealthy man. At one time, he belonged to the entourage of the great Pericles.

At this point, I must mention that our masters at the Academy also gave us a different—and truly divine—pedigree of its founder:

According to one story, Ariston once wanted to possess his wife but was pushed away. Soon thereafter, he saw Apollo in a dream, and thenceforth he never approached Perictione until she bore a son. This son was Plato.

Another story claimed that Apollo had taken the form of Ariston to deceive his wife. Both stories said that Plato was born in the month of *Thargelion*, dedicated to Apollo, and on the day when the birth of Apollo and Artemis is celebrated on the island of Delos.[15]

That's the legend. But when I turn to Plato's writings to find out what he himself says about his father and mother, I find nothing. A man who portrays his friends, teachers, and relatives so willingly seems to be completely silent about those who gave him life.

But maybe I'm wrong. A passage from the eighth book of *The Republic* comes to mind. It is true that the names Ariston and Perictione do not appear in it. It's also true that the situation depicted there is often repeated in many families and repeats itself even today. And yet, when I remember that Ariston was insignificant in public life, while Perictione's brothers and cousins led Athens—a fact of which she must have been as proud as she was of the great names of her ancestors—and as I read these words of Plato, colorful and full of humor, I cannot help but feel that in this fragment he immortalized the portraits of his parents and the fundamental difference of their attitudes.

And so Socrates, discussing a point with Adeimantus,

---

[15] *Thargelia* was one of the chief Athenian festivals in honour of the Delian Apollo and Artemis, held on their birthdays, the 6th and 7th of the month Thargelion (which falls on about our May 24 and May 25).

describes the following situation:

A SON AND HIS PARENTS

An honest man lives in a country with a flawed political system. So he does the right thing: he shuns dignity and does not hold office, nor does he initiate lawsuits. He prefers to do with less and to stay in the shadows so as to avoid all trouble. But the man has a young son who hears as his mother keeps reproaching his father:

"You are a man of no influence. As a result, I mean nothing among women!"

This ambitious wife also sees that her husband is not very concerned about property matters and that he does not attack others and does not get involved either in private disputes before tribunals or in political games but treats all these things with complete indifference. Worst of all, the woman sees her husband constantly lost in thought, and while he shows her no disrespect, he also shows her little interest. This makes her furious. She says to her son:

"Your father is no man! He is a wimp!"

Of course, she adds to these words everything that women like to say on such occasions. Likewise, the servants, supposedly motivated by kindness, secretly whisper something similar in the ear of their young master. So when the household learns that the master is not prosecuting his debtors or even those who accosted him, they advise the young:

"When you grow up, you will get even with those people! You will show them that you are a real man, not a spineless weakling like your father!"

And what does this young man see outside his home, in public life? A similar situation. Those who deal only with what belongs to them are called fools and mean nothing, but others collect fame and praise by meddling in other people's affairs. The young man sees and hears all this. And yet, on the other hand, he is influenced by the words of his father, whose behavior he observes closely. And so he is drawn to both ways of being. The father nurtures and cultivates the rational element of his soul, while others excite lust and wrath in him. The boy is not bad by nature, but he has fallen into bad company. Thus, as a result of the two opposing influnces, he becomes feckless and gives in to ambition and wrath. He becomes proud, he begins to covet honors.

ABOUT HOLDING WOMEN IN COMMON[16]

Wasn't Plato—dreaming of a political career as he was—just like that young man in *The Republic*, in whose heart various reasons and attitudes swirled in conflict? In the opening words of the Seventh Letter, Plato admits to having had such ideas. It seems that he underestimated the modesty and brains of his father, Ariston. It was only after many years of unpleasant experiences and personal failures that he was to pay homage to his way of being. By then, that element of striving and wrath, as he calls it, died out in him, and the element of reason prevailed.

Or did it? Admittedly, after various failed attempts, Plato eventually abandoned his plans for a political career, yet he meditated on the constitution of an ideal state until his dying day. And such thoughts, however excellent their literary form, are also a way of political action and an attempt at shaping the political world! Perhaps even more effective, broader, and more lasting than holding an office or passing a law would have been because the written word knows no boundaries of space and time.

Who can guarantee that someday somewhere, there will not be a community which will decide to implement at least some of the ideas

---

[16] Plato's Republic, the Cynics, and the early Stoics all promoted the abolition of marriage and/or some form of polygamous ideal, and used for it the expression "holding women in common." See Malin Grahn-Wilder, *"Holding Women in Common"—Gender in Early Stoic Utopias,* in In book: Gender and Sexuality in Stoic Philosophy (pp.235-252)

of divine Plato? Even if only those I have already mentioned: that a citizen should be brought up from childhood, by all methods, even on holidays and days of rest and even through the content of poetical works; and that, therefore, such works must be subjected to strict supervision, without shrinking from selection or reworking of old masterpieces so that they could better serve new purposes.[17]

When I think that something like this could one day become a reality, I immediately turn to studying other areas of Plato's theory, such as the problem of demonology. For whatever my enemies say, I personally am deeply convinced that even black magic, even summoning the spirits of the dead, is a lesser evil than certain views which, once uttered, take root in the collective consciousness, grow, and—become flesh.

And yet, here I am in Oea, facing prosecution for casting a love spell! After even if what they say were true, and I had cast such a spell, only the fortune of a wealthy widow would be affected; while Plato's artistic and philosophical magic can easily threaten the happiness of whole nations and whole generations.

But those censors of poetry and music are clearly a joke. For what can one say about the fifth book of *The Republic*? It proposes the establishment of a social class of "guardians," whose job it would be to guide the nation and, therefore, rule the ideal system of the future.[18]

Well, these guardians don't own property. They live together and eat together. They don't even have families. Women of this stratum perform military duties together with men (although theirs are relatively lighter because their sex is weaker). They also work in offices. Marriage does not exist, and parents do not know their children.

------

[17] Something similar, described in Orwell's *1984*, went on in the Old Soviet block where the literary canon was subject to selection and interpretation.

[18] An East European reader would be all too aware that the consitutions of the Soviet-style People's Republics carried the Marxist provision that the Communist Party, an organ self-selected from among the "leading social class" of *proletariat*, was to play a leading role in guiding the state. (And therefore also censoring both present and past books).

The point is that the offspring should be of the best possible quality, and therefore, sexual intercourse is permitted only at the appropriate age. Seemingly, drawing lots determines who will copulate with whom; in fact, however, the rulers—"the perfect guardians"—that is to say the guardians of the guardians—direct the lottery in such a way that the best and healthiest get the best and healthiest mates. These couples then join—temporarily, of course, not permanently— and only at certain festive periods, and the state poets compose appropriate works for this occasion to get the thing going. (Of course,the most deserving guardians shall be rewarded with the special privilege of associating with women outside of this system).

When a child is born, the relevant office will immediately take it away and hand it over to a special unit, where dedicated wet nurses and nannies will take care of it. Mothers may visit these orphanages, but they are not allowed to know which child is their own.

I should also point out that a thought was uttered here indirectly, a monstrous thought—if you think about it: the perfect guardians are allowed to lie and deceive their subjects for the good of the governed. There is no crime that cannot be justified by this maxim.

THE FAMILY OF PERICTIONE

It might seem that I have strayed very far from matters related to Plato's family. But I haven't. Because if we re-read the philosopher's works closely, we notice that they are all imbued with memories of his loved ones and allusions to events and people around him at the time of his youth. Of course, some aspects of the background of his philosophical dialogues are no longer clear to us. Sometimes, however, things are relatively simple. Such is the case with the fifth book of *The Republic,* just mentioned. In it, Socrates talks to Glaucon, Plato's brother, who had come to Piraeus to watch the celebrations in honor of the Thracian goddess. And when he wants to illustrate the principle that in an ideal state, it will be necessary to preselect the parents so that their offspring would be as successful as possible in every respect, he gives an example from Glaucon's experience:

"I have seen hunting dogs and many noble birds at your house. Have you ever been interested in how they mate and reproduce?"

By further probing questions, he easily draws from Glaucon the principal technique of an animal breeder: that one should mate the healthiest animals in their best breeding age, all other breeding being less favorable to the stock. And with all equanimity, both agree that the same principle must be applied to breed the perfect human race.

This fragment of the conversation contributes to the character sketch of Glaucon. The young man, like all his peers from wealthy homes, enjoys hunting small game (because it's been the only game in Attica for centuries) and also breeds birds. Of course, these were fighting birds: their duels were among the favorite pastimes of the Athenians. Plato mentions in passing in his *Laws* that not only children but also some adults exercised and trained their birds by taking them on long walks, carrying them in their hands, or under their cloaks.

Glaucon was named after his mother's father—and here we return to Perictione and her family. I can't prove that the ambitious wife of the peace-loving husband, so vividly depicted by Plato, is Perictione, but it seems highly probable to me. It is certain, though, that her closest relatives were the very epitome of traits diametrically opposed to those of the father of the story; for they interfered in other people's affairs, following the call of greed, lust, and ambition.

Perictione's brother was Charmides, and her cousin—Critias. Both of them played a huge role in the oligarchic government that took power in Athens after the Peloponnesian War. Critias headed the Commission of Thirty, and Charmides sat in the Commission of Ten, which governed Piraeus.

When we remember this, Plato's words about the government of that time—I quoted them before—take on a special eloquence:

"Well, some of them happened to be my relatives and friends; and they immediately began to encourage me to take part in their work, as it concerned me as well."

What kind of activity that was, I have already told you. And it would be easy to point to many other crimes committed by the Commission of Thirty. Still, it's something worth noting that Plato never and nowhere condemned these men. On the contrary, he erected beautiful monuments to both: two of his dialogues bear their names.

THE QUIRKS OF FREE-ASSOCIATION

I picked up the dialogue *Charmides* wishing to reread Plato's characterization of both of his mother's relatives—for Critias also appears in that work. However, while reading the introductory chapter, I came across a discussion that interested me for completely different reasons. It concerns the great mystery of what causes diseases and how they should be treated. Of course, we are not talking about just any diseases, but about that category which is called 'mental.'

This question, always intriguing, was particularly close to me at the time, as living in Pudentilla's house, I observed a very unpleasant case of epilepsy. One of her slaves, a boy named Tallus, was having seizures three or four times a day. He fell to the ground; he foamed, banged his head from side to side, and he looked repulsive. In any case, even when he was not suffering from a seizure, it was hard to call him handsome. His face was pimpled, his eyes were rheumy, his nose flat, cow-like, and his stick-like legs barely supported him. None of the servants would eat with him from a common bowl, none would drink from a pot that he had put to his lips. And as soon as he entered a room, everyone would spit to keep the evil spirit away.

The ways of the human mind are very strange. The divine beauty of the ephebe Charmides, praised in the dialogue by so many people, made me think of the ugliness of poor Tallus. I also reasoned that if there was any disease that could succumb to the treatment recommended by Socrates, it was this disease, so often called 'sacred.' I tried it—and it ended up costing me dearly.

But more on that later. Right now, let me recall that introductory chapter of *Charmides*. It is worth remembering that, according to Plato, the conversation took place before the Peloponnesian War. Charmides was then an adolescent and under the care of his own significantly older cousin, Critias. In this dialogue, as in *The Republic*, Plato makes Socrates the narrator. He had just returned to Athens after a long absence while he served in the army besieging Potidaea.[19] As soon as he arrived within the walls of his native city, he dropped by, as had been his old custom, the Taureas gymnasium, where the flower of the Athenian youth assembled. First, he reported how things went at Potidaea.

CHARMIDES, THE UNCLE OF PLATO

"Then," says Socrates, "I began to ask what had been happening here.

> I inquired about philosophy, how matters stood, and about young people: whether there were any who stood out for their intelligence or beauty, or both. Critias then looked towards the door, for exactly at that moment, a bunch of youths came in, arguing and pushing, with a crowd pressing behind them. He said:
>
> "You will soon see for yourself when it comes to beautiful boys. Because those who are pushing and shoving over there are the vanguard and admirers of someone who is considered the most beautiful these days. He's sure to be nearby."
>
> "And who is he?" I asked.
>
> "You probably know him, though he was still a child when you left. It is Charmides, son of my uncle Glaucon.""I know him, yes, it's

---

[19] Potidaea was a colony founded by Corinth around 600 BC in the narrowest point of the peninsula of Pallene, the westernmost of three peninsulas at the southern end of Chalcidice in northern Greece. Potidaea was inevitably involved in all conflicts between Athens and Corinth.

true. Even then, though still a boy, he seemed quite promising. By now, he must be a young man."

"In a minute, you will see him, how he has grown, and how he looks."

At this moment, Charmides entered the hall.

I'm not much of a judge. I find gold in every beautiful boy, and almost all young people seem beautiful to me. But that day, Charmides seemed like a miracle—he was so good-looking and so handsome. I also got the impression that everyone else was in love with him because as soon as he was in the room, they all lost their cool. And a whole crowd of admirers came pressing behind, too!

Critias turned to me:

"How do you find this youngster? He has a beautiful face, does he not?"

"He's gorgeous!" I replied.

"Oh, but wait till he undresses. You will forget all about the face; his body is so beautiful."

Everyone shouted that it was true. So I said:

"Then no one will resist him. Especially if he is possessed of one more small advantage."

"What advantage is that?" asked Critias.

"If he has an equally beautiful soul. But he must have it, for he is of your lineage."

Critias confirmed this readily:

"Of course! He is perfect in every respect."

"Well, then, perhaps we should bare his soul first. Yes, let us look inside him even before we look at his body. I'm sure he'll agree to talk to us now that he's grown up."

"Let's do that," said Critias. "Anyway, I know he is interested in philosophy. He even has poetic talent. And this is not just his own opinion, but is shared by others."

"My dear Critias, these gifts have long been manifested in your family. You are related to Solon, after all. But show me this young man. Ask him here. He should be able to talk to us without embarrassment in your presence, for you are both his cousin and his protector."

Critias agreed and summoned one of the serving boys:

"Boy, go summon Charmides here. Say I want to introduce him to a doctor. About that ailment of his about which he has been complaining."

And turning to me, he explained:

"He told me that he usually has a headache in the morning. You don't mind pretending to him that you can heal headaches, do you?"

Certainly, I had nothing against a little subterfuge, and I said so.

"Oh, let's hope he comes!"

"He will, for sure!"

And so it happened. He came and caused a huge stir. For each invited him to sit next to him and pushed his neighbor away. One of those sitting on the very edge of the bench had to get up, while another was thrown to the ground.

THE PRESCRIPTION OF ZAMOLXIS

Charmides sat between me and Critias. At that moment, I suddenly felt a strange confusion. All my recent boldness was gone when it had seemed to me that the conversation would be easy. Then Critias said I knew a cure for morning headaches, and the young man looked at me with an indescribable look and prepared to hear my recommendation. All those present in the *palaestra* surrounded us in a circle. I saw the body of Charmides under his cloak. I suddenly had a hot flush and couldn't control myself anymore.

Even so, when he asked whether I knew a cure for headaches, I managed to stammer, though with difficulty, that I did.

"What is it?"

I replied that the cure required a certain herb and also a spell. If one utters the spell as he uses the herb, the medicine will cure him. But without the spell, the herb does not work.

To which he replied:

"So I'll write the spell down!"

"With my permission or without it?" I asked.

He laughed and replied:

"Of course, only with your permission, Socrates!"

"Excellent. I see that you know my name."

"I hope it doesn't bother you to know that there's a lot of talk about you among my peers. I also remember that you used to associate with Critias when I was a boy."

"That's nice of you. And in such case, I am glad to give you the spell. I was just thinking about how I should teach it to you because it is a kind of spell that cures not only the head.

"You've probably heard what good doctors say when someone comes to them complaining of sore eyes. They tell the patient: you can't treat just the eyes. If you really want to heal your eyesight, it is essential that you heal the whole head. And again, it would be a great folly to think that one can treat only the head, ignoring the condition of the rest of the body. According to this principle, they examine the body and try to heal the part along with the whole. You have heard about this, I am sure. Are you ready for such a holistic treatment?"

"Why, certainly!"

As soon as I heard that he agreed to everything, I took heart. Slowly, my boldness returned as well, and the heat of passion enveloped me again.

I said:

"So it's the same with this spell. I learned it from a Thracian during the war at Potidaea. He was one of the physicians of the god Zamolxis.[20] People say that those doctors can even make a man immortal. Well, this Thracian explained to me that the views of the Hellenic physicians, which I have just explained, are indeed correct. But, he went on: 'Zamolxis, our king, who was also a god, prescribed that since one must not treat only the eyes without taking care of the head, or only the head without taking care of the rest of the body, neither must one try to heal the body without thinking about the soul. And exactly this is the reason why Hellenic physicians cannot deal with many diseases: by not paying attention to the soul, they fail to treat the whole man. Because if a man is to do well, all his parts have to be healthy.'

"My Thracian friend explained further that all bodily evil and good begins in the soul and flows from there. So that's why the soul should be taken care of first and foremost! He said finally, my young friend, that the soul is cured by certain spells. And that words of wisdom constitute such spells. For from such words comes self-control of the soul, which is the basis of the health of the whole body.

EPILEPSY AND DEMONOLOGY

Of all of Plato's dialogues, *Timaeus* is my favorite. Of course, I mean *as a source of knowledge*, for I readily admit that it is written in a difficult language and is artistically flawed. The work was created at the end of the divine teacher's life and contains the essence of his views on the creation and structure of the world and man. It also teaches

---

[20] Zalmoxis was a divinity of the Getae and Dacians (people of the lower Danube), mentioned by Herodotus in his *Histories* Book IV, 93–96, written before 425 BC. According to Jordanes' *Getica* (after AD 550) he was a learned philosopher, before whom two other learned men existed, by the names of Zeuta and Deceneus.

what diseases result from various disturbances in the system of elements which make up our body.

Now, Plato attributes the sacred disease—or epilepsy—to a combination of white phlegm and black bile, which arises under certain conditions. This poison then travels up the arteries, reaches the head, and immediately stupefies the reigning spirit, which has its seat in the brain, from where it governs the whole man. The trouble is manageable if this happens during sleep because then the only symptoms are shortness of breath and anxiety. It is quite another story when the patient suddenly loses consciousness and falls to the ground during waking hours, thrashing as if in agony.

But on the other hand, the same Plato teaches us in *Charmides* (through the mouth of Socrates) that all diseases of the body begin in the soul and have their essential roots there. It would seem to follow then that even the sacred disease can be cured by acting appropriately on the patient's psyche. Referring to the Thracian physician, Socrates says that the body should always be healed through the soul and that the soul is most effectively influenced by certain spells, which he says are beautiful and wise words.

It all sounds poetic and sublime, even convincing, but only if you have a handsome boy, Charmides, in front of you as your patient. But the very idea of having a philosophical dialogue with the degenerate moron Tallus seemed to me downright ridiculous. Therefore I considered whether it would be necessary to treat the term "spell" literally, as in performing a magic trick by pronouncing a formula. Perhaps this is what the Thracian doctor had in mind, and Socrates adapted his instructions to the requirements of the moment and the level of the patient with his usual ease?

One fact prompted me to try to heal Tallus.

Plato's writings present an important idea *in utero*, an idea which was subsequently more fully developed by the generations of his successors in the Academy. I'm thinking about demonology. As we know, demons are intermediate creatures between gods and men, circulating in the air zone of our world. From us, they take our prayers and sacrifices to the gods, and from them, they transmit their commands down to us. And therefore, it follows that the divine does not usually come into direct contact with man, neither awake nor asleep. Also, all fortune-telling and all revelations of the future happen thanks to demons. Every man has his demon guardian, which is his protective spirit, and, at the same time, an invisible witness to all his actions and even his most hidden thoughts and desires. After a man's death, the demon immediately seizes the man's soul and carries it to a place of judgment where it confirms or denies his testimony about how he lived his life. And therefore, in essence, what happens to man's soul in the afterlife depends largely on that spirit.

I have long studied the subject of demonology with particular zeal. By diligent reading in the ancient authors, I discovered many interesting testimonies. Thus, these ancient sages said that if given appropriate treatments, young boys easily come into contact with demons and reveal hidden affairs or things yet to come. Here's one example which I find particularly plausible:

It happened in the reign of Emperor Augustus, about a century and a half ago. A large sum of money was stolen from a man. The injured man turned for help to Nigidius, who was at that time famous in Rome for his secret knowledge and enjoyed great authority as a senator and former consul. Well, this Nigidius performed magical rites over a few selected boys, and they revealed where the thieves had buried some of the stolen coins and even where those that had already been put into circulation were located; one of them accidentally got into the purse of Marcus Cato, known for his impeccable honesty.

I've been wondering for a long time but have not been able to establish what kind of boy can make contact with the world of demons more easily: a divinely beautiful, well-born, educated, and universally adored boy like Charmides or a crippled, sick, and downright disgusting slave like Tallus. Both views are supported by equally strong arguments and examples. For, on the one hand, demons, as semi-divine beings, should be particularly eager to seek union with those among us who possess the best mental and physical qualities. But on the other hand—the truth is ancient and well established—that the gods are envious and do not show kindness to those who stand out above the average. So maybe demons look kindly at the handicapped, thus rewarding them for all the pain and suffering of their earthly existence?

After much consideration, I decided that no harm could come to Tallus if I tried to cure him; for who knew if spells and possible contact with his demon might not help him.

And so, I went to my "Charmides."

I TRY TO HEAL TALLUS

I prepared everything correctly. At my command, Tallus presented himself before me in a small, dark room lit by candles which I had set up on the altar. In order to have witnesses that I did nothing other than try to heal him and that nothing untoward was taking place, I invited both Appiuses (with whom I had stayed when I first arrived in Oea) and Pudens, Pudentilla's younger son. The latter's presence was necessary because Tallus was his mother's property. Pontianus was not present as he was out of town.

The ceremony ended very quickly and, to be honest, in complete failure. As usual, Tallus fell to the ground before I could even utter the first words of the spell. I suppose he was terrified by the mysterious scenery. The boy was thrashing about on the floor, foaming at the mouth and mumbling words that were definitely not inspired by demons.

The next day, Tallus was not to be seen anywhere, either in the house or in Oea. I learned from the servants that Pudentilla had sent him to one of her country estates, many miles from the city. However, when I met her, she did not raise the subject at all. It was only at the end of the conversation that she said, seemingly in passing, that she had sent Tallus to the country because the rest of the servants could catch something nasty from him. Of course, I immediately apologized to the mistress of the house for having tried to cure the boy without first asking her permission. I assured her as solemnly as possible that I was guided by pious intentions alone. She said nothing, nodded her head, and smiled mysteriously.

That smile gave me no peace for many days. I kept scratching my head, wondering what it could possibly mean. Didn't she believe me? Could something so small and insignificant have alienated her from me? Unfortunately, Pontianus was still absent: and only he could speak frankly with his mother. Finally, after many days, I had an epiphany. I understood everything. It had to be this:

After the failed healing ceremony, Pudens told his mother about the whole thing, apparently sparing no embellishments. Pudentilla wondered why I wanted to subject Tallus to a spell. She was a prudent and practical woman, so it would not occur to her that noble scientific interests were my only concern. She suspected perhaps that I wanted to achieve something very specific with the rites over the epileptic—perhaps to learn some secret. What secret could that be? Pontianus had been trying to persuade her for quite some time by then that she should marry me. And she knew that I was urged in the same direction. In her eyes, I was a relatively young man, shy and inexperienced, devoted only to science, immersed in ancient books. So she thought it quite natural that I should not have the courage to talk to her on my own about our common cause. And she guessed that I had taken the path of witchcraft because I had wanted to guess my chances of winning her favor. Seen in this light, the whole story could only have flattered her. But there was a different question: I took a sick and disgusting person as an intermediary; and this association may have upset her.

And yet Pudentilla was the first to make a conciliatory gesture. To prove that she was not at all opposed to my studies and that she accepted my explanation about my attempt to heal Tallus, she recommended that a doctor friend of hers bring his epileptic patient to me. Of course, in this case, I didn't even try the rites. I just asked the patient—it was a woman—whether she had a ringing in her ears and in which one more so. She replied that it was on the right.

Thus I was able to overcome my anxiety. Better even, I came out of the whole affair with some benefit: I now knew that Pudentilla favored me. That much was obvious.

I returned to my study of Plato with renewed zeal.

PLATO AND HIS MOTHER'S FAMILY

Socrates' conversation with Charmides eventually led to the question of what constituted *sophrosyne*, that is, prudent self-control (I think this is the best way to translate the Greek word). Critias asserted that Charmides already possessed this beautiful trait of character and that it distinguished him from his peers. To which Socrates politely replied that it was perfectly understandable because the boy came from a great family. His father's ancestors had been praised by Anacreon, Solon, and many other poets. The same was true of Charmides' mother's family: her brother Pyrilampes had once been considered the most handsome man in Athens and, when he served as an ambassador to the Persian king, someone said—on the whole continent of Asia.

I consider the words that Plato put into Socrates' mouth very significant. Charmides, I repeat, was a brother of Plato's mother; thus, by praising his ancestors, Plato paid tribute to his maternal grandfather and great-grandfather. The nod to Pyrilampes is also interesting: Plato's mother married him after the death of her first husband, Ariston, the lover of peace. She thus married one of her uncles. Apparently, Pyrilampes was able to win the love of his stepson since he then wrote about him with such kindness.

It is clear that Plato was deeply attached to his mother's family, although he painted Perictione herself in rather dark colors. He prided himself on the family's ancient tradition and wanted to preserve the most flattering image of his relatives for posterity. The most astonishing thing, however, is that even Critias, the infamous leader of the Thirty, never received a clear condemnation from Plato. On the contrary, in his dialogue *Timaeus*, which I had mentioned above, Critias appears as one of its central characters, while another work of Plato—a continuation of *Timaeus*—is entitled... *Critias*.

And yet he was a man whose actions rightly aroused general indignation. He even tried to ruin Socrates by burdening him with the task of bringing a citizen unlawfully condemned to death to Athens. Somewhere earlier, I quoted a passage from the Seventh Letter, in which Plato, writing about this matter, concludes:

"Of course, the point was to implicate Socrates in their crimes, even against his will. He refused. He was prepared to face any consequences in order to avoid committing an injustice."

It is interesting that Plato uses the word "they"—a collective pronoun: it was his way of not implicating Critias. Plato adored and revered Socrates, but the honor of a family member was also sacred to him. Unable to defend him in this matter, he at least refrained from mentioning his name. But we know that this very Critias was Socrates' chief enemy in the Commission of Thirty. Xenophon, a contemporary of Plato and also a student of the great sage, talks about it openly. I read the story in his *Memoirs*:

CRITIAS AND SOCRATES

Critias was in love with a certain Euthydemus and wanted to satisfy his lust at all costs, while Socrates tried to dissuade him. The philosopher pointed out that it was not proper to behave like a beggar with a man one loves very much and whose respect one wishes to win. However, Critias was deaf to all persuasions. Indignant at this, Socrates said in a large company, and in the presence of Euthydemus himself, something very rude about the conduct of Critias.

Hence the hatred of Critias for Socrates. So when, as the leader of the Commission of Thirty, he introduced new laws, he ordered that the art of rhetoric must no longer be taught because it corrupts the young. This ordinance hurt Socrates, among many others, even though he did not charge for his lessons. Critias, however, could find no other way to attack him, so he accused him of what philosophers are usually accused of in the court of public opinion.

The Commission of Thirty killed many citizens and forced many others to commit crimes. Socrates then said publicly:

"It would be strange if the shepherd of an ailing flock was not criticized for its poor health. But it's even stranger if the leader of a state whose citizens are going to the dogs does not see it and doesn't understand that he's governing badly!"

Of course, these words were immediately reported to the Commission, and Critias and Charicles summoned Socrates. They showed him the text of the law and forbade him from talking to the young. And he, as was his custom, asked modestly:

"Am I allowed to ask you for an explanation of the ordinance?"

"Yes, you may," they replied.

"I am ready to comply with the provisions of your ordinance. But I would like to ask for some additional clarification so that I do not accidentally commit a crime through ignorance. You forbid the teaching of the art of eloquence. Why?"

Charicles raised his voice:

"Since you do not understand this, we will make the ordinance easier to understand: you are not allowed to talk to young people at all."

But Socrates did not give up and continued his questioning:

"To avoid all doubt, you must tell me what young is—up to what age?"

Charicles replied:

"'Young' is anyone who can't vote in the assembly. Therefore, you must not talk to anyone who has not reached thirty."

But Socrates still had doubts:

"This means that if a seller in the market is not yet thirty, I am not allowed to ask him the price of goods he is selling?"

Charicles explained to him patiently:

"In such cases, it is allowed. However, you usually ask a lot of questions pretending not to understand something. So stop asking such questions."

"Does this mean that I should not answer if someone young

asks me, for example, where Charicles lives or where Critias can be found?"

Charicles kept his cool:

"In such cases, you should give the answer."

Critias joined the conversation.

"But you better stay away from all those shoemakers, masons, and blacksmiths of yours. Because I think they must be sick of constantly being a subject of your commentary."

Socrates sought further clarification:

"So, am I also to stay away from the topics which bring up these characters in my conversations: from justice, piety, and all other things of that kind?"

Now, in turn, Charicles pretended not to understand the ambiguity of these words. So he said in a threatening tone, referring to what Critias had said:

"Yes. And also, stay away from the topic of *shepherds*. Because otherwise, it may happen that the headcount of our flock will suffer as a result of your loose talk."

Which Socrates was to understand this way: the population of Athens may decrease by your head.

CONCERNING THE ORIGIN OF RELIGION

Before he gained his gloomy notoriety as the leader of the Thirty Tyrants, Critias enjoyed the reputation of a good poet, a bold thinker, and a capable politician. I perfectly understand that such a personality must have fascinated Plato in his boyhood; for in him, too, both literary and political interests arose early. It is known that he composed dramas and dithyrambs; that he even intended to stage his plays during the festivals of Dionysus in the hope of gaining prizes and fame. But our masters at the Academy say that Socrates diverted him from the literary ambition, which is so common as to be vulgar, and pointed him to a nobler aim: the pursuit of wisdom.

But Plato did not say goodbye to politics so easily. After all, in the Seventh Letter, he honestly confesses that he wanted to devote himself to politics as soon as he came of age. And it seems to me that he remained faithful to his youthful ambitions until the end of his life. And when his attempts at a political career in his own country failed, he tried to implement his ideas in other countries. And in his works, the questions of how to organize a perfect state and how to educate perfect citizens are ever-present.

I confess that these considerations seem irrelevant and uninteresting to me, a citizen of the Empire, the Empire which is the crown and apogee of all nations and all political systems. I mean, is it possible to imagine anything better than the reality in which we have the good fortune to live thanks to the grace of the immortal gods? Yes, people remain as imperfect as they have ever been. However, our constitution is better and more just than Plato could ever have imagined in his wildest dreams. And in his dreams, he had only one city in mind, while our Empire has come to realize its perfection in thousands of cities and hundreds of lands, from the gloomy north to the hot and brilliant south. So I prefer it when Plato talks less about society and education and more about the inner workings of the universe, both visible and invisible, and especially when he talks about demons. For states and their systems come and go, as history teaches; demons, on the other hand, have always existed and will always exist.

Of all of Plato's relatives, only Critias was equally involved in politics and in writing. Of his works, I know only a few fragments. Still, I know that he was a playwright and an author of political treatises in which he discussed the constitution of the governments of Thessaly and Lacedaemon.[21] He praised the latter country above all others and argued that other states should imitate Lacedaemon in every respect. I should mention, therefore, that the ideal political system promoted by Plato is, to a large extent, a development of the assumptions on which the Spartan polity and the Spartan educational system were based. So it would seem that Plato had taken seriously his uncle's views, which

----

[21] Sparta

he must have heard from his own lips.

But enough of politics!

Of the surviving fragments of Critias' work, only one has stuck in my memory. It comes from his drama *Sisyphus*. In it, a person elaborates the following view:

In ancient times, people lived in a beastly disorder and bowed only to force. The honest were not rewarded, and the criminals were not punished. Only later were the first laws established and designed to treat all equally and punish all who transgressed them equally. But these laws only prevented people from committing crimes openly, and evil continued to be done in secret. It was then, I imagine, that some clever and intelligent man first got the idea that men ought to fear gods; for only then would they fear to sin in secrecy, whether in thought, word, or deed. This is how the concept of the deity was invented. This deity was proposed to be an ever-living spirit who hears and sees with the mind alone and who is ever-present; who understands every human word and sees every deed. So even if one plotted evil in secrecy, his actions would not be hidden from the gods, for they have the power to perceive everything. By such arguments, has that man established one of the most ingenious doctrines and imposed falsity on all mankind. He also claimed that the power of the gods comes from the place that at once fills men with the greatest horror and yet is the source of his greatest blessings: the upper air of existence. From there come thunder and lightning, but there the starry robe of the sky spreads out, the life-giving sun shines, and finally, from there the life-giving rain descends upon the earth. In this way, the clever fellow instilled fear of supernatural powers in men, populated the heavens with beautiful gods, and subjugated lawlessness with the fear of god.

GOD AND GODS

Thus, one of Plato's closest relatives was simply an atheist. I have already written that the founder of the Academy himself indignantly rejected such views, although he personally had no particular reverence for any deity and has probably not been initiated into any mysteries. I also cited that chapter in the tenth book of *The Laws*, which I suppose conveys some memories of Plato's childhood years: his mother told him fairy tales about the gods, and his father, surrounded by the whole household, offered sacrifices to the immortals at the home altar on festival days.

But since I have touched on the matters of religion, it seems appropriate to explain briefly the Platonic doctrine concerning the essence of the gods and their place in our world.

The philosopher answers these questions in a dialogue written at the end of his life, namely in *Timaeus*. (We should note that one of the interlocutors in that dialogue is Critias!) The title character of the dialogue—Timaeus himself—a sage and astronomer from the city of Lokroi in Italy, speaks as follows:

There exists an eternal god who created the world: one, material, visible, and built of four elements: fire, earth, water, and air. This world is a living being and contains within itself many other living beings. It has the perfect shape and is therefore spherical, and moves by rotating around its central axis. This world came from the hand of god and is also a deity and has a soul which dwells within him and around him.

God has also created the sun, the moon, and the five planets. He made them out of the element of fire. He placed them on circular hoops around the earth on which they move like on tracks. On the closest rim is the Moon, on the second the Sun, on the third Venus, on the fourth Hermes, and then four other planets follow. And all these bodies, beginning with the Earth, are living and divine beings. Time came into existence only when they were created.

In addition to these deities, there are other deities that we know about through old legends. These deities are the offspring of Earth and Sky; at their head, stand Zeus and Hera, and then follow all the other gods who are so universally worshiped. And the creator god commissioned these divinities—begotten but immortal—to create the bodies of other living beings.

However, the nature of living beings is complex, double. One part is divine and immortal—and it comes from the creator god himself; and the other part is mortal and is the creation of the begotten gods. Now, the creator god made as many souls as there are stars; he settled each soul on a star and showed it a picture of the universe. Later he entrusted these souls to the begotten gods, and they fashioned for them their bodies.

And a divine law was established as follows: that a soul which, while living in the body, manages successfully the conflicting components of her being, will return to her star and will dwell there in happiness. But a soul which succumbs to the temptations of the body will be born again, this time in the body of a woman. And if the soul goes astray yet again in that new incarnation, it will be reborn lower yet, as an animal, according to its misdeeds. Thus being reborn, it will not stop suffering again and again until it is purified by this suffering and returns to the state from which it began its course.

POLYHEDRONS

Continuing with my re-reading of *Timaeus,* I encountered a section of very intricate considerations. It concerns the problem of the shape of the particles of the four elements that make up the world. There, the learned Timaeus first establishes that their shapes must be built up from various triangles—in other words, the faces of these solids must be triangular. He then proves that the particles of fire are four-sided, of earth six-sided, of air eight-sided, and of water twenty-sided.

This whole part of the dialogue seems to me particularly difficult, probably because I myself have never excelled in the principles of geometry and arithmetic. I confess this with great regret, for I remember well that there is an ancient inscription above the entrance to the Academy, supposedly chiseled on the order of Plato himself:

"Let no man ignorant of geometry enter here."

Perhaps this prohibition was observed in the past, but today, I think, most lecturers can not make a correct geometrical proof of some of the more complicated theorems.

Now, as I struggled to understand these chapters of *Timaeus*, Pontianus returned to Oea. He had stayed on one of the family's country estates for some time. I had little inclination to discuss the merits of marrying Pudentilla again, for I had thought through the matter thoroughly. And in any case, since the time of the business with Tallus, a certain thread of unspoken understanding existed between the lady of the house and me, and I was sure we could bring the matter to a happy conclusion without anyone else's help—when the time was ripe. So when Pontianus entered my room, immediately after the first words of greeting, I asked him how he understood Plato's teaching on the structure of the elements, especially how he imagined these solids with triangular sides. Pontianus also did not have a clear picture of geometric figures but found an unexpected solution. He said that here, in Oea, a craftsman—part carpenter, part sculptor—made such strange objects with fancy shapes in his workshop.

We immediately went to him to see if we could find anything resembling the *Timaeus* polyhedrons.

THE MYSTERIOUS BUSINESS OF THE STATUETTE

The workshop of Cornelius Saturninus was located in a narrow, dark side street. It was open to the outside. The proprietor, a thin old man with a penetrating gaze, sat on a low stool just outside the entrance. He was diligently fiddling with thin boxwood slats.

I froze, rooted to the ground, when I saw his intricate works set on the table by the wall. There were various figures known from geometry, both flat and three-dimensional, some with rounded and others with flat faces. There were also sculptures, some tiny, others quite large, depicting gods, people, and animals. Indeed, it seemed that Saturninus could shape wood like clay! Although we did not find anything in the multitude of his works that corresponded exactly to those particles described in *Timaeus*, we understood at once that this master could easily represent any polyhedron made of triangles in wood.

Full of admiration for the talent and skill of this humble craftsman, I became engrossed in a conversation with him, though he was not a talkative man. I asked him whether he could build for me a rather fancy machine; it was a kind of mechanical toy, but it had a serious, scientific purpose. I developed the design while still in Madauros, but I could not find a suitable artisan there to make it. Meanwhile, Saturninus immediately understood what I meant and how this device was supposed to work, even without a sketch. I sensed that he enjoyed this type of work immensely because it required a great deal of skill and wit. He not only agreed to build it quickly but also asked whether I needed a statue of some deity.

As if he were reading my mind! But just as I was getting ready to answer him, Pontianus interjected:

"And why would you need such a statue? Don't we have enough figurines of gods at home? And, in any case, if we were to fashion a new figurine, I would prefer a statuette of metal, not of wood!"

I explained to Pontianus that I had been accustomed to carrying a likeness of the divinity with me. That I used to put it in the room where I worked and worshipped it, and that on feast days, I burned incense before it. And when I was tired of mental work, I sought my rest in it. But, when I left Madauros, I did not take my statuette with me because I hoped to reach Alexandria soon and acquire something appropriate there, something truly Egyptian, sacred, and in the ancient style. Finally, I allowed myself a little lecture, not without the hope of pleasing the master:

"As for the material of which the statuette is to be made, one should always keep in mind the teachings of Plato, given in the twelfth Book of *The Laws*. There is talk there that when offering sacrifices to the gods, it is proper to observe moderation. And so, since the earth and the hearth are already consecrated to the gods, there is no need to sanctify them to the gods again. In many countries, objects made of gold and silver decorate private homes as well as God's shrines, but expensive metals cause envy and covetousness and lead to discord, and are therefore not fit for worship. And ivory comes from a dead animal, so it is not a pure gift, either. Finally, we must not forget that bronze and iron serve as tools of war. And therefore, what material to use? Therefore, he who desires to make a truly pleasing offering should use the most modest of materials and, for that very reason, the most appropriate: either wood or stone!

Saturninus was clearly pleased with this argument. So as we were leaving, he said :

"I will make you a very beautiful statuette of Mercury."

I was struck speechless. After all, I had not told him which deity's statuette I desired! But, in the secrecy of my heart, I really had been thinking about Mercury-Hermes. Perhaps Saturninus had guessed it because the god has been worshipped from time immemorial and in all civilized countries as the protector of poets and philosophers? Maybe. But who knows, perhaps the mysterious master woodcarver could read other people's minds?

MEETING RUFINUS

We only managed a few steps before Herennius Rufinus barred our way. Fat, bald, filthy, he greeted us with effusive cordiality, although in truth, he only knew Pontianus well. He had seen me once, I guess, after my public oration at the basilica. It was easy to guess why he sought our company—of relatively young and wealthy men; for all Oea had been gossiping with glee about this man and his domestic affairs.

He can be described briefly: a cantankerous and pugnacious fraudster, slanderer, intriguer, glutton, libertine, and a thoroughly depraved person. Even as a boy, he willingly served all kinds of wickedness. As a youth, before his baldness disfigured him, he performed on theater stages, dancing in pantomime plays; and he danced—those who saw them told me—as if he had no tendons or bones: a pure shapelessness without art, sloppy and primitive. There is an opinion out there that the only thing of an actor left in him was his shamelessness. When he came to a mature age, his house became a house of iniquity. His wife is a whore, everyone knows it, and his sons learn from their father. Day and night, hooligans kick at his gate and sing lewd songs in the street. Drunks in the dining room, cuckolds in the bedroom, the arrangement between the spouses is widely known: he who gives his wife a nice gift is free to come and go as he pleases, and no one will stop him. But if anyone dares to come empty-handed, at a given sign, the servants catch him as a seducer. And he won't leave the "hospitable" house until he proves he can sign his name.

But I think we must take pity on the poor man. What else can he do since he has already squandered all the fortune he inherited from his father? And the latter, indebted up to his eyeballs, had always preferred money to honor. Creditors were constantly after him, and when he went out into the street, almost every passer-by tried to catch him. Finally, he announced insolvency. He came to terms with some of his creditors and discarded all pretense of personal dignity. But before he did that, he had first transferred most of his fortune (with the help of an extremely cunning legal trick) to his wife. From then on, he lived as a poor man, possessing nothing except his own disgrace. But he left his son, Rufinus, three million; for so much did the son inherit from his mother's estate. All this, however, Rufinus managed to go through in only a few short years—as if he feared others might think that he inherited something.

Finally, the day came when his wife, no longer in her first youth, announced that she would no longer support the whole house. It was necessary to look for a way out of poverty. Since the daughter was already grown up, the good father decided to marry her off to someone wealthy. He offered the girl—this was loud all over the city—to all the wealthier bachelors. Apparently, some of them even got her on a trial basis.

So it was quite clear what intentions he had in his heart when he began to embrace and kiss us in that narrow street in front of Saturninus's workshop.

THE SKELETON AND THE KING

Our new friend's eagle eye soon espied which establishment we had just left. So he started to ask what we had been doing with this oddball Saturninus. He added, in a half-whisper and with a very significant expression, that he could tell us a lot about him because he is a very uncanny man.

Rufinus was, of course, trying to draw us into a conversation and build up our curiosity, which he could then direct to his own purposes. Although I was interested in the person of the extraordinary craftsman, I preferred to get rid of the disgusting man. So I made up a fairy tale:

"Oh, yes, we know all about that. That's why we have chosen him. For we have just ordered from him the figurine of a wooden skeleton. With such a figurine in hand, all one has to do is pronounce some appropriate spells, and one gains power over the dead."

Rufinus looked at me incredulously but also with a shadow of fear. He'd probably heard something about my studying philosophy and maybe even some rumors about me trying to cure Tallus of his illness. Oea is not a big city, and whatever happened in one of the most distinguished houses soon became common knowledge. But Rufinus was a tough case and not so easy to get rid of. He took my words seriously and eagerly took up the topic:

"Oh, yes, I have heard about that. I have a friend here in Oea, his name is Crassus. Every year, he spends a few months in Alexandria.

He's there right now. Well, not so long ago, he showed me a gold ring bought in Egypt from a high priest (or so he says). There is an image inscribed upon it: a standing lion, with the royal sign of Isis in place of his head and his right paw resting on the skull of a supine skeleton. Crassus swears that the ring has miraculous powers, not just of healing but also of making a man invisible. And the mysterious sign supposedly reads "the king of the skeletons."

At this point, Pontianus, wishing to show off his knowledge of the subject, lectured us on the symbols and terminology used in the occult sciences. Such a skeleton, if it is made from the right wood, bears the name of "king," which is *basileus* in Greek, and this because he rules over all deities and all living beings. In closing, he added politely:

"But the wood must be special, rare, and expensive. Not your ordinary boxwood. Ebony would be the best. I'll see to it for you, Apuleius. I know a matron who owns an ebony box."

By then, I had had enough of this conversation, even though it was fun to watch Rufinus's face; for he did not know whether we were mocking him or whether we openly confessed to practicing grim magical rites. We had by then reached the forum. I said that I still had to visit an acquaintance, said goodbye, and quickly walked away. I felt a grudge against Pontianus. For by speaking of "the king," he made a clear allusion to one of the most secret teachings of our Academy. Plato himself expounds on it only in the form of symbols in his Second Letter. There, he writes to Dionysius:

"You say that the nature of what is called 'The First' has not been sufficiently explained to you. It is, therefore, necessary to tell you about it, but with symbols, so that should this letter be intercepted along the way, the uncalled-for reader would not understand what it says. As regards the king of all, all things are his, and all exists for his sake, and he is the cause of all that is beautiful. In relation to the 'Second' everything is secondary, and in relation to the 'Third' everything is third."[22]

---

[22] R. G. Bury argues that the Second Letter is almost certainly inauthentic,

On the other hand, as I walked, I reflected that Plato had been fond of telling parables about miracles and magic and also about rings that give their owners extraordinary powers. Of course, such parables always served to illustrate some great universal principle. Such is the case in the second book of *The Republic*, where Glaucon, the brother of Plato, actually develops ideas consistent with the atheist theories of Critias, who had thought that the all-seeing god was only invented to keep people from wrong-doing.

THE RING OF GYGES

Glaucon made a bold assertion. He probably did it against his own convictions, perhaps out of contrariness, but mainly in order to get Socrates to explain his views. Glaucon's argument went as follows:

People act justly and honestly only because they do not have enough strength and courage to do what they really want to do and what would really benefit them.

While giving different arguments in support of his thesis, Glaucon cited a legendary story:

Centuries ago, a simple man named Gyges lived in Lydia. He served the king of that country by tending his flocks. Once upon a time, there was a heavy rain, followed by an earthquake. Just where Gyges stood, the ground split and a chasm opened up, showing an entrance to an underground cave. The shepherd boldly ventured inside and saw something strange: in the cave, there stood a huge horse of bronze with a trap door in his torso. Gyges opened it, looked inside, and saw the corpse of a giant. The corpse was completely naked but had a beautiful ring on his finger. The shepherd took it off and brought it back into the daylight.

---

based primarily upon conflicts between it and Plato's Seventh Letter. Bury's own conclusion is that its tone and content are decidedly un-Platonic. R. G. Bury (trans.), *Works of Plato: A New and Literal Version, Chiefly from the Text of Stallbaum,* vol. IV

Soon after, all the shepherds in the area gathered together to count their flocks and report to the king. Gyges sat among his companions as usual. By chance, playing with the ring (or perhaps trying to hide something so precious from them), he turned the gemstone within it. To his amazement, he realized that his companions started looking about and asking where Gyges had gone. They talked about him as if he were absent and were surprised that he disappeared so suddenly. So after a while, he turned the stone again and immediately became visible. Thus he found the ring to have miraculous properties and began to consider how he could use them.

He undertook the mission of reporting to the king on the health and headcount of the royal flocks. But once inside the palace, he used the ring's special power. First, he seduced the king's wife, then together with her, he murdered the king and seized the throne for himself.

From this story, Glaucon drew a general conclusion. He said:

"Suppose there are two such rings in the world. One of them falls into the hands of an honest man, the other—those of an ordinary scoundrel. I'm sure they'd both benefit from the magic power in the same way. After all, even the most honest man in the world would not resist the temptation: to be able to do anything he wants with complete impunity! So he would enter every house and take whatever he pleased. He could also kill freely and suddenly and free people from prisons. He would have the power of a god."

Therefore, Glaucon came to this conclusion:

The ring of Gyges, if it really existed, would prove that everyone prefers to act dishonestly as long as he can avoid responsibility.

THE GOVERNMENT OF CRITIAS

Once in power, Critias acted as if he had the ring of Gyges. He feared nothing, cared for nothing, least of all for public opinion. He stood—

or thought he stood—above good and evil. I have given enough examples of how tyrannical the Commission of Thirty was. He tried to tie Plato, a member of his family, to himself as closely as possible. Of course, Plato could not join the Commission or the Council because he was too young—he was only twenty-four, but he was probably proposed some unofficial but important functions. Plato initially hesitated. This is clear from the words of the Seventh Letter, which serve as a kind of justification:

"It is not surprising that I was under some illusions at the time: I was very young, after all. It seemed to me that this government might lead our country from misrule to the rule of law. Therefore, I carefully watched how the new rulers would act."

Plato's hesitation is understandable. Democrats who formerly led the state had committed many crimes, both in domestic and foreign policy, and they bore chief responsibility for the defeat of Athens in the war. It was, therefore, widely expected that the new government would learn from the obvious mistakes of the previous system and act more reasonably. It should also be remembered that the Committee of Thirty initially did not use excessively harsh methods. The terror grew only gradually. But in its final stages, its victims were no longer just ordinary citizens and residents of Athens but even Commission members themselves. Critias caused the destruction of his ruling colleague, Theramenes, a supporter of the moderate faction. His downfall was public. The assembly to which Theramenes had appealed remained deathly silent for fear of the thugs of Critias and the swords of the Spartan garrison. No one protested as the unfortunate man was torn away from the altar where he had claimed divine asylum and dragged across the square to prison in broad daylight, where he was obliged to drink hemlock.

Afterward, Critias ruled without any regard for pretenses. He persecuted even the wealthy and sentenced to death completely innocent people. The total number of the murdered was, as I have already said, over fifteen hundred. About five thousand sought refuge outside Athens. Most refugees gathered in Thebes. At their head stood a fellow named Thrasybulus.

And how did Plato react to these events? He himself says that what upset him most was the effort by the Thirty to force Socrates to collaborate in their crimes. The Seventh Letter then adds in general terms:

"I looked at all this and other things—many as important—and was overcome with disgust. I resolved to keep away from the evil taking place in our city. But soon afterward, the rule of the Thirty ended, and the regime fell."

Thus, in just one short sentence, Plato summarizes the extremely dramatic events that took place in Athens in the second year of the 94th Olympiad [403 BC]. And yet they also affected his family, and very painfully, too. Perhaps that was why he preferred not to dwell on the tragedy?

THE INSURGENTS OF PHILAE AND THE MASS MURDER IN ELEUSIS

At the beginning of winter, a group of seventy emigrants, led by Thrasybulus, secretly set out from Thebes and crossed the mountains into the lands of Attica. Here they captured a small fortress at Philae. It lies on the slopes of Mount Parnassus and is only half a day's journey from Athens. On hearing this, the Commission of Thirty immediately led three thousand heavily armed infantrymen and a cavalry detachment out of the city. Only those citizens whom the Commission could fully trust served in the army.

It would seem that the force was powerful enough to crush the handful of daredevils with one blow. But as the soldiers moved towards the walls of the fortress, a hail of bullets and arrows rained down upon them. The attackers withdrew, carrying many wounded. Despite this, no one doubted that the annihilation of the insurgents was only a matter of time and a short time at that. In order not to expose its people to unnecessary losses, the Commission decided to surround the fortress with a rampart and thus cut it off from supplies

However, after the previously beautiful weather, at night, there came a sudden change, and it began to snow. The unprepared soldiers, standing under the open skies, suffered severely from the cold. It was therefore decided to abandon the construction of the ditch for the time being, and the army returned to the city. During the march, they suffered some losses because the insurgents made a bold raid on the wagon train and seized many of their pack animals.

(Here, I must make an observation. It seems to me highly probable that Plato's brothers, and perhaps he himself, took part in the expedition against the insurgents. For they were all of military age, had considerable family wealth, and were closely related to the leaders of the Commission).

After this first setback, the Commission sent Spartans and some cavalry to Philae. This unit set up camp in a nearby town, and from there, it intended to cut off the supply lines of the insurgents. Meanwhile, many people from the area had already joined Thrasybulus: he now had about seven hundred men under his command. At night, quietly, he descended at their head from the mountain fortress, and early in the morning, he struck the enemy's positions taking the Spartans by surprise. The attackers killed about a hundred and twenty hoplites and a few horsemen. The rest escaped in a stampede all the way to Athens. Of course, the government immediately sent additional forces against Thrasybulus, but by then, he was already safely within the walls of the mountain fortress.

The failure made the Commission anxious about the future. Fearing the worst, they decided that it was necessary to prepare in advance a place where they could retreat and defend themselves in the event of a revolt in Athens. The choice fell on the temple precinct at Eleusis, which was spacious and surrounded by defensive walls. As I have already said, the place lies not far from Athens, about half a day's journey. Around it stretches a fertile plain, surrounding a beautiful bay. Critias left for Eleusis immediately and deceitfully imprisoned all the adult men of the town. He brought them to Athens, imprisoned them, and then summoned all the three thousand wealthiest citizens (who were the voting mainstay of his regime) to the great concert hall—it's called the Odeon and had been built by Pericles. He told them with brutal candor:

"Both we, the members of the Commission, and all of you are interested in the maintenance of the current system. Hence the obvious conclusion is that you must bear your share of the risk. It is your duty to order that the prisoners of Eleusis be put to death because then the responsibility will rest upon us all equally."

An open vote was held. Since armed Spartans soldiers were waiting in another part of the Odeon, the result of the vote was in line with Critias's wishes.

And now, a question arises in my mind: how did Plato's brothers vote? They must have been present at the assembly, for they were over thirty years of age. In any case, the crime committed by Critias against the inhabitants of Eleusis would explain why Plato was never initiated into the Eleusian mysteries.

THE BATTLE OF PIRAEUS

Sometime later that spring, Thrasybulus gathered about a thousand men about him. From Philae, he moved against Piraeus. He entered the port under the cover of darkness and took control of it. But his force was too small to defend the entire perimeter of the walls. So, when the army of the Thirty arrived from Athens along with the Spartan garrison, the insurgents withdrew onto the hill of Munichia.[23] That is the hill on which the temple of the Thracian goddess Bendis stands and where the annual processions and night horse races with torches take place. As I described above, this celebration was once admired by Socrates and Plato's brothers and perhaps by Plato himself.

The men of the Thirty stood in tight, deep ranks in the Piraeus market. There were many more of them than of the insurgents, but

---

[23] Munichia or Munychia is the ancient Greek name for a steep hill (86 metres (282 ft) high) in Piraeus.

they were in a worse position: if they wanted to attack, they would have to attack uphill. This made them more vulnerable to sling-bullets and arrows. Besides, the insurgents were also favored by the local population, who, for lack of other weapons, pelted the oppressors with stones. When it came to battle, the troops of the Thirty were not brave. Of these, only seventy fell, but both Critias and Charmides were among those killed. The rest fled in terror.

The victors behaved very chivalrously. Only weapons were taken from the dead. Soon there arrived from the city the relatives of the dead to collect the bodies. There must have been someone from Plato's household among them, maybe even he himself, since giving the last service to the dead was one of the most sacred duties of a Greek family.

And so this was the new situation: Piraeus was now in the hands of Thrasybulus, while Athens remained under the power of the Commission and its henchmen. However, the mood in Athens was so foul that the following day the Thirty decided to flee the city. They left for Eleusis, that sacred precinct which Critias had so foreseeably prepared for them, and a new Commission, the Nine, was appointed in their place.

So now there were three governments in Athens: the democratic rebels in Piraeus, the oligarchic government of the Nine in Athens, and the tyrannical regime in Eleusis. This condition lasted most of the summer. There was no more fighting between their main forces, but both sides, those in Piraeus and those in Athens, made occasional forays into the surrounding countryside and there were sporadic bloody skirmishes between them.

Only then did Lacedaemon decide to intervene in the Athenian affairs. Spartan troops entered Attica. Had they attacked the insurgents in Pireus at once, Thrasybullus would have had to surrender. However, two factions clashed within the Lacedaemonian government, fueled by mutual animosities between King Pausanias and the more experienced general Lysander. Since the latter strongly demanded that Thrasybulus' movement be crushed as soon as possible, King Pausanias defiantly sponsored a compromise agreement between Athens and Piraeus. The terms were simple: democracy was to be restored throughout the country, but no one would be held accountable for acts committed in the past—except those who had been members of the Commissions of Thirty, Eleven, and Nine. And thus, for the first time in the history of Athens, a political amnesty was announced.

In the fall, the insurgents from Piraeus entered Athens as victors. They first ascended the Acropolis, where they offered a thanksgiving sacrifice to the goddess Athena, the protectress of the people and the state.

PLATO AND THE DEMOCRATS

For Plato and his family, those months were full of unsettling tension and anxiety. There was mourning in the house because of the death of their relatives. Later, there was the fear that the victorious democrats might go back on their solemn oath and seek vengeance for all the misdeeds of the Commission of Thirty, imprison and exile supporters of the old regime, and confiscate their property. In that case, Plato and his brothers would be among the first to suffer, for they were the nephews of Charmides and Critias.

However, no one was hurt. The Democrats kept their word. Aristotle, writing the history of Athens several decades later, characterizes that period in the following way:

"Both individuals and the community behaved so beautifully in the face of past misfortunes and with such reason as nowhere and never else. For not only did they obliterate from their memory the transgressions of the past, but they even paid back to the Lacedaemonians the money which the government of the Thirty had borrowed for the war, though the original agreement was that each side—the oligarchs from the city and the Piraeus insurgents—was to pay its debts separately. But they decided that the main objective was to maintain peace and harmony, whereas, in other cities, the victorious party never pays its debts and often forces a land redistribution.

Likewise, three years later, they reached a compromise with those citizens who had removed to Eleusis, thus ending the civil war."

Plato, a witness to the events, does not seem to have been as enthusiastic about the new government as Aristotle was. However, taking into account his specific family situation, it should be recognized that the restrained words of the Seventh Letter are still very eloquent:

"So again, although not as strongly as before, I was tempted to participate in political life. Yet, it was a time of turmoil, and many things remained to be indignant about. It is not surprising that in the midst of a dramatic change, some took revenge on their enemies. However, those who then returned to the city exercised great restraint."

So Plato hesitated, watched, and waited. On the other hand, he was all the more willing and eager to associate with Socrates.

A SUNNY DAY BY THE RIVER ILISOS

Soon after the overthrow of the Thirty, Lysias returned to Athens—that same Lysias whom I have already described: the son of Cephalus and the brother of Polemarchus who had been sentenced to death by the Tyrants. Lysias, arrested in the days of terror, survived only by sheer luck. He fled first to Megara and from there to Syracuse, where his family had come from. He now tried to recover their confiscated property but failed.

Lysias had become a respected lawyer and a famous master of rhetoric. He introduced to Athens certain legal tricks and methods of argumentation which had been invented in Syracuse. The local audience, still unfamiliar with the new kind of eloquence, was impressed. Groups of friends and admirers of Lysias gathered in various private homes, warmly receiving his speeches and readings.

The subject of one of the speeches was a very paradoxical statement: that a young man who is the object of love should choose not an ardent admirer but, on the contrary, someone who sincerely confesses that he is not in love. The argument was clever, subversive, and—shallow. Nevertheless, one of the young listeners, Phaedrus, left deeply impressed. He managed to get hold of a copy of the speech and, straight from the master's performance, went for a walk outside the city walls. He wanted to sober up after this intoxicating experience and read the wonderful speech once again. Besides, Phaedrus had been listening to Lysias since early morning, and it was now afternoon, and it was time to take a little walk. And since he agreed with those who recommended resting not in the streets but in nature, he followed the road leading out of the city.

There, he met Socrates. The old man soon got out of him from where he came, to whom he had listened, and where he was going. And so, they went together, for Socrates was also curious about Lysias' speech. Walking along the River Ilisos, they looked for a place to sit in the shade. At last, they came to rest under a mighty sycamore, a great tree visible from far away. Nearby a beautiful willow sprinkled with fragrant flowers hung her tressed down. Next to the sycamore, a spring flowed. Socrates touched the water with his foot: it was very cold. All around, there were many statuettes of nymphs and other deities. A gentle, cool breeze carried the song of crickets. The lush grass spread before them, inviting them to stretch out.

Socrates praised the place with such delight that Phaedrus was surprised:

"What an extraordinary man you are! You speak as if you have arrived from very far away and were not a native Athenian at all! Indeed, it seems to me that you never leave the city walls!"

Socrates excused himself gently. He always excelled at the graceful use of polite words, though sometimes he sounded a little ironic. And now he said something important:

"I want to learn all the time, and yet the land and the trees cannot teach me anything. Only the people in the city can."

When he had finally settled comfortably on the grass, he at once asked Phaedrus to read the speech of Lysias to him.

This is the beginning of the Platonic dialogue entitled

Phaedrus—from the name of that young man. Like all other people appearing in Plato's works, this figure is a real person, although he never amounted to much in the history of Athens. Phaedrus was probably a contemporary of Plato; he was one of his friends, he associated with Socrates, he knew many eminent people. It seems, however, that because of his genteel interests in literature and art, he completely neglected the care of domestic affairs. For I read in a certain court decision that he had become a poor man; he was saved from utter poverty only by marrying a girl who brought him a sizable—though not exorbitant—dowry.

Plato does not appear in any of his dialogues as an actor. The artist modestly remains in the shadow, although he was one of the people closest to Socrates in the last years of his life. Instead, he puts his relatives and friends in the foreground: a beautiful tribute to their memory. In many cases, however, it is difficult for me to resist the impression that Plato, in setting the background and scenery of his dialogues, used very personal memories. I have already spoken of this in connection with the beginning of *The Republic*. Here the matter is a little more difficult, and I certainly cannot prove it, but I have the feeling that it was not Phaedrus but Plato himself who spoke to Socrates on a fine summer's day on the banks of the River Ilisos at the foot of a tall sycamore tree where a cold spring flowed.

The days were happy days of summer, of peace.

I DRAW ADVICE FROM PHAEDRUS

The beautiful Greek name Phaedrus can be loosely translated as "Radiant." Therefore, whenever I imagine the figure of this friend of Plato, I see a young man shining with beauty, with the grace of movement and the splendor of intellect. But when I now realized that this charming ephebe, alive with the brilliance of poetry and the subtlety of philosophical inquiry, in later years was forced to look for a woman with a meager dowry because he had not done well himself,

I immediately realized: why, I had walked the same path! My studies in Athens, my travels in Greece, my stay in Rome, my current trip to Egypt—have all taken a serious toll on my finances. I was still considered rich, true, and in a way, I was. The fortune inherited from my father in Madauros was large, estimated at three million sesterces. However, it carried a mortgage because I had to take out various loans to raise the necessary cash, and the income from the land was not enough to cover it; the interest piled up, and the debt grew. The fate of Phaedrus made me realize how close to danger I was.

I told myself:

My life's goal is to explore philosophy and the occult sciences in order to make contact with spirits and to elevate myself to godhood. Not for me the pleasures of the table and the bed, not for me the joys of family life. My duty is to work, study, and mortify the body and the soul. It does not follow, however, that I should renounce in advance the advantages offered by a wisely-administered, well-furnished house. Of course, if I took a young wife, she would be a source of trouble and anxiety. I would have to serve her, take care of her outfits, tremble whether she does not cheat on me perhaps, father children.

But things would be different with Pudentilla. She is an experienced woman, she already has offspring, the affairs of the bed are important to her only insofar as they are necessary for health. Nobody will seduce her. I can see that she manages the house excellently. Why, then, should I not place in her hands the care of the troublesome trifles of my daily life? In Madauros, my old freedwomen, whom I inherited from my parents, are looking after my property. They will steal for sure. And I have no way of even checking that they are not exceeding all reasonable bounds. After all, it is impossible to simultaneously study Plato and walk around the market and ask the vendors how much dried fish and greens cost today.

As for the matter of property, this is what I thought:

The dowry doesn't have to be much. In fact, I don't even have to receive it in cash. It is enough if the money is secured by my wife's estate. The house in Madauros could be liquidated, I would move here with all chattel. I would then cover the cost of living and studies from

Pudentilla's income.

For some time, I was still worried about going to Egypt. I did not want to give up this plan because I treated the journey as a pilgrimage in the footsteps of Plato and Pythagoras. However, I remembered in time what Rufinus had said about his acquaintance—that Crassus. That man, living in Oea, spent much of each year in Alexandria. It was a good idea, worth emulating. After all, it wasn't far from here to the capital of Egypt—if you walked along the coast of Great Sirte.

A REPRESENTATION OF THE UNIVERSE

Lost in such profound mediations, I did not even notice that Cornelius Saturninus, the carpenter artist from whom I had ordered a statuette of Mercury and a certain device a few days ago, was standing at the door of my room. He entered, holding in his hands a large, though not very heavy object, covered with a cloth. He placed it on the table and, with obvious pride, almost theatrically, pulled the cover off.

I clapped my hands with joy. Here was before me a model of the cosmos, made just as I had dreamed it and as I had explained it to Saturninus.

The globe hung in the air, supported on a horizontal metal rod fixed in a tall, carved vertical stand. Through the globe, vertically, ran a kind of axle in the shape of a very elongated spindle with eight concentric hoops of various diameters mounted upon it. The largest of them, the outer one, marked the heavens of the fixed stars. The hoops were successively smaller and smaller, and on each, a planet revolved: Saturn, Jupiter, Mars, Mercury, Venus, the Sun, the Moon. And they all revolved around the immobile ball of our Earth.

I had seen similar devices in Athens and Rome. And I undertook my journey to Alexandria to buy or order from a good craftsman just such a representation of the cosmos. After all, it is well known that the science of the heavens still flourishes in Egypt, thanks to the old schools of Egyptian priests, the great Greek library, and the scholars working there. Never in my wildest dreams would I have imagined that I would find such an excellent craftsman here, in Oea, not the most famous of towns.

Of course, the model was not completely accurate. For, surely, no mortal could ever reproduce with ordinary materials and with ordinary instruments what Plato describes at the end of the tenth book of *The Republic*. There he tells us the story of Er, a son of Armenia, who, wounded in battle, lay unconscious for many days among the slain. Found and presumed dead, he was about to be burned on a funeral pyre when he regained consciousness at the last moment. And that Er, while he lay unconscious at the doorstep of death, saw with his own eyes the fate of human souls in the afterlife, and observed the structure of the universe, which he described like this:

The great Axis of Necessity runs through the whole cosmos and pierces the Earth, which sits in the center of it. Around it, there are eight concentric circles, or perhaps spheres. The first sphere, the largest, envelops the entire universe as if a cloak; the inner spheres move, but they have different angles of rotation and different speeds. The course of the eighth, innermost, or lunar sphere is the fastest; slower, but always the same, rotates the seventh, solar, and the sixth and fifth: Hermes and Aphrodite. Each celestial sphere has a different color. The first, the outermost, twinkles with thousands of stars; the seventh burns most intensely, while the eighth only glistens with reflected sunlight. And finally: each sphere has its siren, which travels with it and sings in a different voice, but all their melodies are interdependent and together form a divine harmony.

This picture of the cosmos is relatively simple; in reality, however, the movements of the planets seem very complicated and apparently difficult to calculate. Plato devotes more space to this in *Timaeus*. There, he states broadly that it is impossible to describe the processions of planets, their mutual meetings, and the intersections of the tracks on which they run. And so, even in *Timaeus,* the master does not go into details and does not reveal the secret of planetary revolutions. So why should I require that Saturninus, a smart but unlearned man, represent in a wooden model what even the words of the founder of the Academy could not measure up to?

I know that today's Alexandrian astronomers can say a lot about the ways of the planets. They probably look at models like mine with indulgent smiles. But who can guarantee that twenty centuries from now, the views of our scholars will not be regarded as erroneous and naive? Perhaps by then, men will have formulated other hypotheses, fuller and more accurate. For no one has the right to say about himself: I have penetrated in the smallest detail the plan of the Demiurge, the creator of the universe. All that we see is but a shadow and a partial reflection of the eternal order. This is what Plato always taught, and I never understood his words so clearly and naturally as I did at that moment when I first saw the ball and hoops of boxwood arranged by Saturninus's hand.

I thought to myself:

True, it is a very imperfect and simplified picture of the cosmos, but still, it is its likeness! I must therefore contemplate it and venerate it in the same way in which I contemplate and venerate the statues of the gods. After all, it is Plato who indicates that the whole universe is a god, living and immortal. Its parts are also divine beings: the planets revolving on their tracks and the globe itself. The statues of the gods of Olympus all represent figures we have never seen. And yet, those gods were created only in the second place, after the divine celestial bodies. Therefore, it is necessary, first and foremost, to pay homage to what is first, more powerful, more eminent, even if the representation of the eternal order of the universe appears in a form as modest and fragile as the work of an Oean craftsman.

PLATO AND ASTROLOGY

I asked Saturninus how he managed to carry out my commission so quickly and faithfully. He replied that this work gave him great joy because he had long been interested in the stars and the sky and that he was convinced that they had a powerful influence on our affairs and even foretold our future. He himself did not know the secrets of this science. He had only heard something of it from visiting astrologers who cast horoscopes in the forum. But he highly valued my wisdom and knowledge because I had studied philosophy in Athens. It had also come to his ears that my speech, delivered a few months ago in the city's basilica, had been widely praised.

I was flattered by his words, though they came from a simple man. How was I supposed to reply to him? I have never studied the principles of astrology and have some doubts about the methods used by many of its practicioners. Simply put, it seems to me that their customers hear from them exactly what they want to hear. And how easy it is to see through the motivations and schemes of common people! And in the few less clear cases, it is not too difficult to dress the horoscope in an ambiguous form. But I do not condemn astrology in its entirety, for I know that it has been held in high esteem for millennia in the lands where many arcane arts had originated.

I am also always intrigued by a certain passage in Plato's *Timaeus*. It speaks of the complicated movements and processions of the planets; about how they meet and drift apart; that there are conjunctions and oppositions; about the fact that sometimes one of them will overshadow the other. And then comes this sentence:

"And in this way, they send warnings and signs of the future to those who can't reason."

Perfectly clear. Plato looked with pity on people who wanted to guess the future from observing phenomena such as the motions of the planets or their eclipses because he believed that all those phenomena happened as a consequence of certain immutable laws and were, therefore fully predictable by calculation. And yet, in some manuscripts, the same sentence reads:

"And in this way, they [that is, the stars] send warnings and signs of the future to those who *can* reason."

And in this case, it would seem, we have here the praise and justification of astrology! There is no consensus among the masters of the Academy on the correct version of the text; there are supporters and opponents of each.

Meanwhile, Saturninus kept talking. He began to tell me what his neighbors were whispering about: that Rufinus, whom I had met in front of his shop, had been asking an astrologer about his daughter's marriage. He received the answer that the girl would marry soon but then quickly be widowed, inheriting great wealth from the deceased.

"But how can that happen?" I asked. "Once this heavenly decision becomes known, no one will dare marry Herennia!"

Saturninus disagreed:

Rufinus's conversation with the astrologer had been overheard by one of the servants. And it would be a good thing if many people heard of it, for if Herennia did marry after all, and then the rest of the prophecy came true, who would dare mock the astrologers again?

I didn't like Rufinus, I didn't care about his daughter, and the whole conversation seemed frivolous to me. On the other hand, I did not want to dismiss Saturninus too hastily, lest I appeared too puffed-up with conceit, one of those who will never devote a moment of their precious time to a simple man. Anyway, I have to repeat that I really liked this craftsman.

So to turn our conversation to different, more worthy topic, I asked, pointing to the model of the cosmos:

"You made the model in such a way that the hoops can rotate forward or backward. Why?"

Saturninus, probably a little hurt, began to excuse himself:

"Of course, I know perfectly well that the circle of the sky rolls only from east to west, but it would be very difficult to make a model which can rotate in one direction only. I'll try to think about it some more."

Immediately, I consoled him:

"But I don't want that at all! You did very well. Because the rotation of the universe does not always have one direction, the one to which we are accustomed. It sometimes takes the opposite direction."

"How do you mean, the opposite direction?" cried out Saturninus, sincerely surprised. "I have never heard such a thing!"

Bosschère

"Because only true philosophers who diligently study Plato's teachings know about it. Listen to what he teaches in his dialogue entitled *The Statesman*."

THE GREAT TRANSFORMATION

This happens very rarely, at intervals of several thousand years, but happen it does! The cosmic ball suddenly stops and then starts to spin in the opposite direction. This phenomenon is, of course, connected with a terrible cataclysm, which causes the majority of life on earth to perish, humans first and foremost. Yet some creatures, including a few humans, persist, and they witness something strange. What it is, is hard for me to imagine, let alone describe: time itself goes backward.

All past events now repeat themselves but in the opposite order and direction. To put it simply: who at the moment of transformation was an old man with gray hair, gradually transforms into a mature man, then into a youth, then into a boy and a child, and finally re-enters his mother's womb. What's even more amazing: people who have already died reappear and start the retrograde path of life. They emerge from the earth, rise from their graves, their ashes and bones grow together anew. There is no birth, only resurrection.

This is what Plato says. I have given you his words in a nutshell. However, a close study of this story leads to interesting conclusions. First of all, you must wonder what happens in the minds of those people whose life now runs backward (from our perspective). Probably you suppose that they are shaken, that they live in some monstrous fear and terror. No such thing! They are just as calm and normal as we are today. They behave normally. They believe that everything is happening as it should. For consider that since the world and time now go backward, the memory of man is completely wiped out. People now know their future, but they know nothing of their past. They are like wanderers who do not remember where they have come from and what hardships they have left behind, but see clearly and in all detail the road stretching before them. Such a situation seems to them not only normal but sensible. They cannot imagine how things could be any different. Suppose, however, that someone reveals to them our way of life. They would surely be surprised. They would ask:

"Holy sandals, what is this backward-looking existence? No one knows what will be but instead remembers what was? Why? Surely, familiarity with the future is both necessary and salutary, even if we cannot change it, while the memory of things past has no meaning at all. What has passed is gone, will never come back, we cannot change it. Why bother?"

We could persist and answer them:

"It would be monstrous to know the future in every detail and not be able to change it one iota! It would be better to die now since you already know what you're going to do in a moment, in a year, in twenty years; since my every gesture, every word, even my every thought is already set, why bother going through with it?"

It follows that man, no matter which way the world turns, will never be happy and satisfied. Only the gods control the past and the future.

I don't know how much of my words the worthy master woodcarver and admirer of astrology understood. But he listened very attentively, almost reverently. That was not surprising: he probably heard Plato's words explained to him for the first time in his life: the words of a true philosopher. And I, who related those words to him, was probably, in his eyes, the most eminent sage in the world. I must admit that I felt very flattered.

But I had grown a little tired of those intellectual heights, of dealing with the Demiurge, the creator of the cosmos, and these considerations of the rotations of the sphere of the universe. I longed for contact with historical events, even very remote but concrete and attested. So it was with some pleasure that I now returned to the story of Plato's life.

We had left him in Athens, which, after the overthrow of the

Commission of Thirty, became a democracy again. They were happy, beautiful, and free years, like that sunny summer day when Socrates and Phaedrus sat talking in the shade of a sycamore tree on the banks of the Ilisos, talking about Lysias's masterful speech.

But the bucolic weather was misleading.

THE EXPEDITION OF CYRUS

Shortly after the democratic revolution, a foreigner arrived in Athens who, despite his young age—he was only twenty years old—easily found access to many great houses. His name was Menon. He came from Thessaly and belonged to the most prominent families of the local aristocracy there. He was very handsome, intelligent, enterprising, curious about foreign countries and people, and eager for adventure. He stayed in Athens only briefly, for he was on a long and dangerous journey, and he hoped that it would open up a glorious future for him and earn him fame and fortune in the fairy-tale lands of the East.

His story was as follows:

The Persian prince Cyrus, governor of Asia Minor, had sent agents to Greece to recruit soldiers. He did this secretly but with the tacit approval of the Spartan government, which had the most to say in Hellas. Cyrus planned to form a large mercenary army and march at its head against his brother, the king of Persia, Artaxerxes, to overthrow him and seize his throne. Of course, the prince kept the purpose of his armaments in the strictest secrecy. Officially, there was only talk of a punitive expedition against some recalcitrant people in the mountains of Asia Minor. But the agents of Cyrus gave all to understand that if all went well, the mercenaries would earn booty and fame beyond their wildest dreams. Therefore, in various countries of Hellas, thousands of volunteers applied. That was hardly surprising: the land had recently been devastated by a long war, there was general hunger and unemployment.

In Athens itself, Cyrus's recruiters accomplished little. There was, however, one young man who seriously considered whether he should go into the service of the Persian prince. That young man was Xenophon. He was less than thirty, one of Plato's peers, and, like Plato, he came from an old Athenian family. Thus, Plato and Xenophon had much in common; plus, both were hostile to democracy. Above all, however, they were brought together by the person of their common teacher, Socrates.

Xenophon was encouraged to take part in the expedition by an old friend of his family, Proxenos. He had spent much time with Cyrus in Asia, and from there, he sent a letter saying:

"When you come to us, I will introduce you to Cyrus, whom I love more than I love my country."

Xenophon asked Socrates for advice, and he said:

"By associating yourself with Cyrus, you will offend our government because, during the last war, Cyrus was on the side of the Spartans. So it is best for you to go to Delphi and ask Apollo. Then you can say you're only following the god's instructions."

And this is what Xenophon did. He turned to the oracle and asked:

"Which god should I sacrifice to? To whom should I pray for a successful trip so that I return to my homeland healthy and whole?"

He received an answer and returned to Athens satisfied. However, Socrates was displeased and reproached Xenophon:

"You have decided to go on that journey all by yourself! You should have asked god which was better: to go on the expedition or to stay at home, and not asked, as you did, how to prepare for the expedition! But now that you've done that, you must follow the god's command."

And thus, Xenophon offered sacrifices to the gods whom Apollo had indicated and left for Asia. It is possible that he traveled there with Menon, whom he must have met in Athens.

The story of Socrates' advice seems to me credible because Xenophon recorded it in his memoirs. They clearly show how close he was to the sage: he considered himself his disciple and repeatedly stressed this in his later writings. How often, then, he had to have come into contact with Plato! They came from the same social class, lived in the same milieu, studied at the feet of the same master, were surrounded by the same friends. And yet, Plato never mentions Xenophon in his writings, as far as I remember. And vice versa: in Xenophon's memoirs about Socrates, Plato's name appears only once, and even that—in passing.

Did the two dislike each other?

MENON AND XENOPHON

But let me go back to Menon and his stay in Athens. I understand perfectly well that the Thessalian aristocrat, radiant with the charm of youth, attracted the attention of Socrates and his friends. It was easy to meet people in the gymnasium, where men gathered daily to practice and chat. Socrates often spent whole days there. And most likely, it was there, in the gymnasium, that a conversation took place, which Plato was to remember for the rest of his life. He immortalized it years later—of course, reworking it his own way—in a dialogue, to which he gave the title *Menon*, for Menon appears in it as its chief interlocutor.

The discussion is devoted to a subject to which Plato returns in his work, namely, the question of whether *arete*, that is, virtue or excellence, can be the subject of instruction or whether it is an inborn gift. The dialogue does not give a definite answer, but it contains many clues for further consideration.

In his work, Plato characterizes Menon indirectly:

He is a young man, proud of his beauty—beauty confirmed by a large circle of his admirers. Like every representative of the aristocracy, he considers wealth, honors, and high offices to be the highest goods in life. For his times, he is a well-educated man: he is well acquainted with poetry and appreciates the master of sophistry, Gorgias. He often takes part in philosophical discussions.

But Xenophon, who perhaps knew Menon better and

longer—for they had taken part in Cyrus' expedition together—gave him the worst possible testimony. He wrote that Menon was motivated above all by the desire for wealth and power, and to achieve them, he was ready to resort to any means, even fraud and perjury. He supposedly stated openly—if Xenophon is to be believed—that only a fool respects truth and honesty, and he only showed kindness to those against whom he was plotting. He kept away from people like himself—liars and deceivers—preying mainly on the naivety of simple-minded people. He boasted how clever he was in tricking people, and he called those who could not do the same 'losers.'

This image does not seem convincing to me: it is too exaggerated. For it seems to me that a really clever man never brags about his cunning but, on the contrary, pretends to be a simpleton. Yet, if Xenophon is to be believed, Menon acted with the overt cynicism sometimes seen in young people, arrogant and sure of themselves. The undisguised passion emanating from the quoted character sketch leads me to suspect that Xenophon perhaps hated Menon. Perhaps, there had been some quarrel between them during the expedition. It may have begun with a quarrel that broke out between the men of Menon and Clearchus[24] on the banks of the Euphrates; it came close to a bloody fratricidal fight. And Clearchus was one of Xenophon's closest friends. Thenceforth, they both regarded Menon as their enemy.

Yet, years later, Xenophon tried to convince his readers that the real reason why he judged Menon so harshly was different, deeper, and rested on objective facts. They, too, are related to the fate of Cyrus' expedition.

Cyrus attacked the armies of his brother King Artaxerxes on the plains of Babylonia. He won, in part thanks to the courage of his Greek mercenaries, but he himself died in battle. The Greeks were left without a leader, surrounded by an impenetrable host of enemies, in the heart of a hostile country. Seeing no other way out, they began negotiations with the king's dignitaries. During these negotiations, the

---

[24] Clearchus: a Spartan commander in Cyrus's army

Persians treacherously captured the Greek officers and immediately murdered them. This did not bring the expected benefits to the Persians because the Greek soldiers refused to surrender. When they recovered from their shock, they took a desperate step. Sword in hand, they broke out of the encirclement and marched from the plains of Babylonia to the north. They marched through the high, snow-covered mountains of Armenia while defending themselves against the constant attacks of the enemy. Finally, overcoming all dangers and hardships, they reached the coast of the Black Sea. There, the coastal Greek cities helped them return to their homeland.

Xenophon was one of the commanders of this retreat of the "ten thousand," and he wrote an account of these extraordinary events. Describing the dramatic moments immediately after the battle, when talks with the Persians started, Xenophon claims that Menon communicated with the enemy behind his companions' backs and was ready to deliver them into Persian slavery. But this appears to me to be mere slander. After all, the Persians deceitfully captured Menon along with the other Greek officers. And although he was not beheaded at once like the others, he suffered an even worse fate.

Menon was imprisoned and tortured for a whole year. He was probably killed in the Persian manner: gradually, by having his hands, legs, and ears cut off and his eyes gouged out. He died like a thief, says Xenophon contemptuously, as if with satisfaction. But his cruel judgment seems to have been isolated. The news of the young man's martyrdom shocked the many Athenians who had recently hosted him. Plato was certainly one of those sorely afflicted. He never forgot Menon and made his name and figure famous for all time.

The Thessalian aristocrat died in the far east, probably in the second year of the 95th Olympiad [399 BC]. And in the same year, his Athenian interlocutor, Socrates, also passed away from the world of the living.

ANYTUS ON THE EDUCATION OF THE YOUNG

Only two people take part in the discussion of the *Menon* dialogue: Menon and Socrates. At some point, however, a third figure appears on the scene. Socrates puts it this way:

> Anytus joined us at the right moment. He seemed the perfect person to ask for an opinion. First, he was the son of a wealthy and wise man, Anthemion, who became rich not by accident and not thanks to someone else's gifts but earned everything himself through ingenuity and hard work. And yet, he was not arrogant, proud, or overbearing, as often is the case with self-made men, but calm and helpful. Equally importantly, he had raised and educated his son Anytus properly. At least, that's what people in Athens thought because they elected Anytus to the highest offices of the state. I thought that it was smart to involve such a person in our inquiry on the subject of whether any teachers of virtue could exist.

And thus, Socrates questioned Anytus. If Menon aspired to become a doctor, a saddler, or a flute player, he would be sent to study with a doctor, a saddler, or a flute player. But Menon claims that he wants the sort of knowledge that would allow him to manage his home and state well, respect his parents, and behave properly towards fellow citizens and foreigners. To whom then shall we send Menon, which teachers had such knowledge? Perhaps to those who offer to teach such things for money? Should we send Menon to the Sophists?

But Anytus shouted with alarm :

"Say no such thing, Socrates! May none of my family or friends commit such madness! For it is obvious that Sophists spoil and corrupt every one with whom they socialize."

Socrates pretended surprise:

"How can that be? So they not only do not help, but they cause harm? And in exchange, they dare to take money? I find it hard to believe. I know that the Sophist Protagoras earned more by this skill than Phidias, the excellent sculptor. Indeed, more than ten Phidiases taken together. If a shoemaker or a tailor took shoes or a coat for repair and returned them in a worse condition, the thing would be known at once, and he himself would soon die of hunger. Meanwhile, Protagoras has managed to hide from all Hellas that he corrupts those who associate with him! And for forty years, too! Because I believe he died when he was about seventy, and he practiced his art for the greater part of his life. Even more strangely, he always had an excellent reputation and still does to this day. And not only he but also a lot of other Sophists, both older and younger than him. According to you, then, shall we say that they deliberately deceive and corrupt the young? Or are they simply unaware of it? In either case, it would amount to saying that men generally revered as wise are actually—madmen!"

Anytus replied with deep conviction:

"They are not madmen! The young people who pay them are. And even bigger madmen are their relatives who allow this. But the greatest fools of all are the states which allow Sophists to practice their trade and do not drive them away!"

Socrates asked with paternal care:

"Has one of those Sophists hurt you?"

Anytus was indignant:

"No! I have never had anything to do with any of them! Nor would I ever allow anyone of my people to!"

"Does this mean that you do not have any personal experience with any of these people?"

"And I hope I never do!"

"Then how can you, dear Anytus, know anything about the activity of the Sophists, whether good or bad, when you lack any experience of them?"

"Easy! I know their sort! All are the same, whether I know them or not!"

"You must be a seer, Anytus! For how else could you have formed any idea of the matter? But let us no longer inquire what these Sophists are like—these men who would so grossly corrupt our Menon. If that's what you say, we shall accept your opinion about them. But then, would you show to our guest to whom in this great city he should go in order to acquire the civic virtues he desires?"

"And why don't you point them out?"

"I have already said: I would send him to those who claim to be such teachers. But apparently, I said something unwise, or at least you think so. And maybe you're right. But you tell us: to whom among the Athenians should our Menon turn? Give us a name!"

"Why only one name? Any honest man he meets in Athens will certainly influence him better than all the Sophists combined."

But Socrates did not yield:

"But did these virtuous and good people become so by themselves? Didn't they learn from anyone? And if they have, can't they shape others in the same way?"

"I think they learned from others who were also virtuous and good. I think you will agree that our city has never lacked such people."

Socrates replied with all seriousness:

"I think, Anytus, that we have many good politicians and that we have had many before, too. But were they able to pass on to others the civic virtues they possessed? Because this is what we are discussing and not whether there are in our city virtuous and good people. Or have been in the past. We are trying to figure out whether civic virtue can be taught."

GOOD FATHERS AND BAD SONS

At this point, Plato—still speaking through the mouth of Socrates—goes on to discuss a matter that often recurs in his works: apparently, this problem seemed to him of particular importance. The essence of this issue can be summarized as follows:

Everyone agrees that Themistocles, Aristides, and Pericles, the greatest leaders of Athens of the recent past, were good politicians and good citizens. It is also widely known that they cared greatly for the education of their sons. They spared no effort and costs. They provided them with the best teachers they could find in various skills, such as riding, music, gymnastics, wrestling. It seems clear that these fathers also wanted to pass on to their sons their political wisdom. They would certainly have taken every step to make that happen. Yet that is precisely what they failed to achieve: their sons never amounted to anything in political life. Neither did the fathers inculcate civic virtues in their sons, nor did they secure for them good civics teachers. The conclusion is simple: *arete*, or civic virtue, cannot be taught. You have to come to it by yourself, by your own effort.

The answer given by Anytus to this long argument of Socrates is significant:

"It seems to me, Socrates, that you find it easy to talk badly about people. And I would give you some advice if only you would listen to it: be careful. In all countries, it is easier to harm a person than it is to help one, but in ours, it is especially easy!"

Socrates did not answer the warning of Anytus but instead turned to Menon:

"It seems to me that Anytus has become angry. I am not surprised. He probably thinks I'm accusing those great politicians and probably includes himself in their number."

And thus, the scene with Anytus ended with the sharp accent—of a threat on the one hand and a contemptuous remark on the other. Three years later, Anytus was among those who accused Socrates in court. The old man was accused of disrespecting the state religion, of introducing new gods, and of corrupting the youth.

A PORTRAIT OF ANYTUS

Anytus' father had become rich through his own enterprise. Socrates says this clearly: "by his own work and ingenuity." He founded a tannery workshop, which was then inherited and run by Anytus. So, unlike Critias, Plato, or Xenophon, Anytus was not an aristocrat and probably did not own any landed property. He belonged to a class that got rich by running various types of commercial enterprises. Athens, the capital of the Maritime League, offered great opportunities to people with initiative. The field was so broad that even foreigners were encouraged to settle there. And thus, Cephalus, the father of Lysias and Polemarchus, had come to Athens from Syracuse at the urging of Pericles himself. He opened an armorer's workshop and soon became a very wealthy man.

Yet, I find a lot of evidence in the literature of the time that the Athenian aristocracy—members of the old landowning families—looked on these wealthy men of commerce with undisguised distaste. Aristophanes' comedies love to mock the sausage makers, shoemakers, and tanners who presume to involve themselves in politics and aspire to positions of leadership.

And that was Anytus' ambition, too. Having an assured existence and adequate financial means—thanks to his father's industry—he could think about a great career. He associated himself with democrats. For a time, he was a follower of Alcibiades and even, I suspect, an admirer of him. He then joined the board of *strategoi*.[25] Commanding one of the armies, he suffered defeat in a battle with Sparta, though not through his fault. In some strange way, he managed to save himself from the anger of the people and was not prosecuted, as used to happen in Athens in similar cases. I think he just bribed the judges. When the Commission of Thirty took power after the Athenian defeat, Anytus, as a democrat, went into exile. He returned from it with those who had taken the fortress of Philae: he belonged to the closest entourage of Thrasybulus. It is, therefore, understandable that after the final victory of the democrats, Anytus found himself among the most influential politicians.

However, when I read the words with which Socrates presents Anytus in *Meno*, I detect a distinct note of irony:

"His father brought him up and educated him properly. Or at least that's what they think in Athens."

---

[25] In Classical Athens, the office of strategos existed already in the 6th century BC, but with the reforms of Cleisthenes in 501 BC, it assumed its most recognizable form: Cleisthenes instituted a board of ten *strategoi* who were elected annually. The ten were of equal status, they decided on strategy by majority vote, and each held the presidency in daily rotation.

The further development of the conversation shows very clearly how justified that note of irony was. Anytus revealed himself as ignorant and impudently arrogant to boot. For he admits that he is an enemy of the Sophists, though he has never known one. He says with the confidence so typical of simpletons:

"Oh, I know their sort! All are the same, whether I know them or not!"

Of course, Plato deliberately introduced this motif into the dialogue. He wanted to show that the man who would accuse Socrates in the near future was apt to make unjust judgments without thinking and without any reason, motivated only by an aversion to educated people, which often characterizes the lower orders.

Whereas about the father of Anytus, Socrates says:

"Nor was he arrogant, proud, or overbearing, but calm and helpful."

But these qualities he failed to pass on to his son and thus did not bring him up properly, contrary to what the majority of Athenians thought of Anytus. Soon, however, it turned out that he was not the only one who could not properly educate his offspring. For when Anytus argued that civic virtues could only be learned by associating with the right people—a view that is perfectly understandable in a democrat—Socrates reminded him that even the most famous politicians had been unable to raise their own sons. Anytus did not reply to these words with any rational argument but became indignant and threatened the old man. Why? Of course not because he thought himself among those who had been unable to learn *arete* from their fathers.

No.

Anytus felt slighted as a father.

Concentrated entirely on his own career, he did not take care of his son. Socrates once pointed this out to him:

"Since the state bestows upon you the highest dignities, is it fitting that your son should be brought up in a tannery?"

But he had a good opinion of the boy. He said once to one of his friends:

"I met him once. We spoke briefly, but it seemed to me that he had a strong personality. That is why I say that he will not endure the life of a tannery slave, which his father has assigned to him. And since he has no one to guide him, he will be carried away by some base passion and will become depraved."

Which is what happened. Anytus's son turned to drink and achieved nothing in life.

CONCERNING THE HELMSMEN OF THE STATE

Anytus was not the only man to be rebuked so severely by Socrates. The philosopher publicly pointed out all kinds of faults and shortcomings of many people he encountered. He didn't care about their position or influence, he did not think at all about the consequences of their anger. I have already described how sharply he denounced the greed of Critias. It wasn't just individuals, however. In the last years of the war with Lacedaemon, he alone had the courage to oppose the will of the whole people, which, prompted by a clique of cynical politicians, demanded the death of several generals.

The generals were being prosecuted for having failed to give a proper burial to Athenian soldiers who had fallen in a victorious naval battle. It proved useless to explain that a terrible storm broke out immediately after the battle, and one had to think not about burying the dead but about saving the remaining fleet. The plebs, deaf against all arguments, followed its leaders and demanded an immediate vote, bypassing the basic rules of procedure. Only Socrates, then a member of the assembly, opposed this resolution and demanded proper legal procedure. Unsuccessfully. The assembly voted. The accused were sentenced to death, and the sentence was carried out. Later, remorse came, and everyone regretted what had happened. Of course, that regret didn't mean that Socrates' position came to be considered correct. On the contrary, the opinion of him as a stubborn weirdo who always worked against everyone—because he presumably despised all men—only gained currency.

Socrates also criticized certain political institutions, which in Athens passed for the pinnacle of democracy. One of these was the principle that candidates for some higher offices were selected by lot. The old man pointed out:

"Where is the man in the whole wide world who would be guided by fate in choosing a craftsman? And yet, if a craftsman does something wrong, the damage is comparatively small. But how great is the damage when the helmsman of the state makes a mistake!"

And thus, Socrates openly said to individual politicians that they were not mere fools but dangerous fools because they proposed to lead the state and the community. He pointed out the same ignorance and overconfidence to poets and writers. Nor did he forget, when the occasion arose, to mock the craftsmen: because each of them, knowing perfectly well his job but only that, was at the same time deeply convinced that he should and was able to speak out on every issue, especially on political matters.

And Socrates allegedly did the same to the god Apollo: he claimed that, despite his divinity, he was fallible. This concerned a case which, if Plato is to be believed, Socrates presented in his defense speech.

SOCRATES AND POLITICIANS

You all still remember Chairephone. He was my friend and a good companion to many of you. He went with you into exile during the tyranny of the Thirty and returned with you to Athens. You probably remember how Chairephone was: how bravely he went about whatever he set his mind to do. Well, one day, he went to Delphi and boldly asked the oracle—and please do not start a racket when I say this—he asked if there existed a person in the world wiser than Socrates. To this question, Pythia replied: 'There is none!' And that this was really so, this brother of Chairephone will testify to us, for Chairephone himself has passed away.

Now, when these words of the oracle were reported to me, I thought to myself:

"What is god actually saying? I know I am not wise, certainly not very, or even a little. So what does god mean by saying that I am the smartest? Because he's obviously not lying, he can't!"

For a long time, I could not understand what god had meant. Finally, I set about finding an answer. I used this method:I went to someone who had a reputation for being extremely smart. In this simple way, I wanted to disprove the oracle's claim and demonstrate to god: behold, there is a wiser man than me, so you must be mistaken! I began to observe that man closely and talked to him often. I prefer not to mention his name, but it was a certain politician. And what happened? Very quickly, I came to the conclusion that while this man *seemed* wise to many, and especially to himself, in reality, he was not wise at all. So I tried to show him that he had a false idea of himself. Unfortunately, the result of my efforts was that I attracted his hatred, his and that of his friends. So when I got home, I thought:

"I'm smarter than that politician. For although we both do not know what beauty and goodness are, he thinks he knows, although he does not, while I do not know either, but at least I do not think that I know. So it seems I'm smarter than he by at least this much: I don't think I know what I don't know."

SOCRATES AND THE YOUNG

Thus began the old man's journey in search of wisdom among the inhabitants of Athens. His search won him—as he frankly admits— the heartfelt hatred of a multitude of Athenians, people of various classes and professions. Among the enemies of Socrates were members of the intellectual elite of the time, and it was no accident that Meletus and Lycon, a poet and a rhetorician, brought formal charges against him and that the politician Anytus joined them.

But there were other reasons for resentment and suspicion of

Socrates. This is what he said about it:

"Young people accompany me everywhere of their own free will. Of course, those that have the time, that is, those from the homes of the rich. They find it amusing to watch me question people in order to discover if they are wise, and they often imitate me and try to investigate this or that themselves. And we find whole hosts of men to whom it seems that they know something though they know little or nothing. But those who are tested are angry with us and not with their own stupidity. And they say wherever they can: 'Look at that great fool, Socrates, the corrupter of youth!' But when someone asks them what this Socrates is doing or saying, they can't say anything sensible. However, lest it should appear that they lack information, they bring up what philosophers are usually accused of: that I am talking about what is in heaven and what is in the netherworld; or that I do not believe in gods; or that I teach how to prove black white and white black."

Such were the words of Socrates. But I think that matters were probably not that simple.

This "testing" of serious people by self-confident youngsters must have caused many disputes, misunderstandings, insults, and much anger. After all, it is easy to imagine that most of the interviewees saw in their interlocutors nothing more than arrogant teenagers, their heads turned by an old fool. Moreover, a great many of those offended were right! For how many of those who imitated Socrates were able to do so with his tact and wit? Not everyone is able to understand the difference between simplicity and rudeness and the line between directness and insolence.

It was also a matter of who these young people were. Socrates himself had to admit that those who gathered around him were mainly the sons of the rich, the golden youth of Athens of his time. That alone was probably enough to set the lower classes against him. Worse still, many of those youths who at various times associated with Socrates made a poor impression on the public, for they were cynical, capable of any crime, ruthless both in politics and in private life. It is enough to mention Alcibiades and Critias. Not everyone knew that there had been a violent quarrel between the leader of the Thirty Tyrants and Socrates. Few witnessed the beautiful scene when the old man refused the order to go to Salamis and arrest a sentenced man and bravely went home instead. The older people, on the other hand, remembered well that Socrates had often talked with young Critias and marveled at the beauty of his nephew, the young Charmides. And when Critias and Charmides died, Socrates' circle included their closest relatives: Plato and his brothers.

THE PROTECTIVE SPIRIT AND POLICY

Socrates argued with many people, old and young. He discussed fundamental questions concerning the entire community.

"But it might seem odd to you," said Socrates in his defense speech, "that I speak about such things only privately and do not have the courage to appear publicly before you. About my reason for this, you have often heard from me. Behold, sometimes something happens to me by the will of a deity or of a protective spirit. This started happening when I was still a boy. It is a kind of voice. It speaks to me to prevent me from doing something, but it never tells me what to do. This voice that forbids me from engaging in politics. And I think it's very wise to forbid it. For you know well that if I had turned to politics, I wouldn't have been of any help to you or myself and would have perished long ago. Don't blame me for telling the truth: every man who opposes his community out of honesty and who tries to prevent evil and lawlessness must perish. Unfortunately, this is how it is: whoever wants to work for a just cause and yet live at least a while should avoid politics."

Perhaps Socrates said something like this in his speech before the Athenian court. On the other hand, it seems to me that Plato's personal experience also emerges from these words: bitterness, aversion to politicians like Anytus—and such people always seem to win!—and the growing conviction that he will never achieve anything in politics. I can believe that a protective spirit kept Socrates from participating in political life. But it seems certain to me that Plato's protective spirit said the same to him—either his protective spirit or simply his common sense. All this is clear from the very harsh and personal tone of the Seventh Letter.

Plato wrote it in his old age. As he did, he thought back to those gloomy months when the Athenian democrats had prosecuted Socrates and put him to death. He relived the pain he had felt at that time—pain due to the death of his teacher, yes, but also due to the fact that he had to give up his own political ambitions yet again:

"It happened that some influential people charged our friend, Socrates, bringing against him the most wicked charge, and one totally improbable in his case. So they accused him of impiety, and the judges sentenced him to death. They killed a man who bravely refused to take part in the criminal abduction of one of them while they—these democrats!—were trembling for their lives in exile."

FASTER THAN DEATH

None of his accusers had a clear idea of the content of Socrates' teachings. How many of the judges—mostly simple peasants and craftsmen—could understand that he was not a creator of any philosophical or religious system? And that he wanted, above all, to know how to learn the truth?

But his accusers knew the mood of the plebs. They knew perfectly well how suspicious it was of all novelties and all educated people. So they didn't inquire too deeply. They simply accused Socrates of what has always been imputed to all philosophers in history: impiety. Impiety and sowing confusion among the young, that is, "corrupting them."

I must remind you that the Athenians were not just a religious society—they were superstitious. The case brought against Socrates was not the first of its kind. Several other trials against philosophers had been held in Athens in the preceding decades. Just before the Peloponnesian War, an attempt was made to charge the old man Anaxagoras with impiety. He had been a teacher of Pericles, but despite such high protection, he had to flee the city. Some years later, Protagoras of Abdera was charged and convicted on impiety charges. He was one of the most talented Sophists and was held in high esteem throughout Hellas. The books of Protagoras were publicly burned. He saved himself by escaping to Sicily, but his ship reportedly sank on the high seas. A few years later, the books of Diagoras of Melos—also allegedly godless—were burned in Athens. Their author went into hiding in the Peloponnese while Athenian heralds proclaimed throughout Hellas a prize on his head.

Unlike those unfortunates, Socrates did not run away, although his accusers probably expected he would. He remained in Athens, appeared before the court, made a defense speech, or what we call an *apologia*, bold and even offensive in tone. He was sentenced to death and sent to prison to await execution. He could have escaped from there. His friends raised enough money to bribe the guards— everything was for sale in Athens. A considerable amount of time must have elapsed between the sentence and the execution since no one was allowed to be put to death before the return of the sacred ship sent to the island of Delos to the sanctuary of Apollo. So there was plenty of time. And yet the old man stubbornly rejected all avenues of rescue, even though he knew that a small gesture was enough to save himself. In his last words before the court, he said:

"Every dangerous situation offers many ways to avoid death as long as one is prepared to stop at nothing. Really, it isn't hard to escape death. It is much more difficult to escape evil: evil is faster than death."

In the spring of the second year of the 95th Olympiad, Socrates drank a pitcher of hemlock.

A KIND OF DIZZY SPELL

I will not give you a long-winded account of the death of Socrates here. Nor will I recount the conversations he had with his students and friends while in prison, awaiting his execution.[26] All of this has been recorded for posterity by Plato in his two dialogues, *Phaedo* and *Crito*, though he himself, apparently due to an illness, was not present at his master's side. Nor will I try to describe Plato's reaction to the news that the old man, his beloved, had died. He probably cried—like they all did, young and old, gathered at his bedside. They watched, shaken and powerless, how the jailor touched his numb legs and factually explained:

"When the poison reaches his heart, he will die."

Rather, I will go straight to the topic of my work. Let me remind you in the words of Plato—words taken from the Seventh Letter—what his thoughts were in the period immediately following the death of Socrates, which he felt had testified to a deep disease of the political system and perhaps of the whole society:

"I looked at all this and at the politicians of the time, and, as I advanced in years, the more I considered the laws and customs binding our society, the more difficult it seemed to me to take part in state affairs. On the one hand, it was impossible to break in without the help of friends and faithful companions; but those whom I had known were no longer around, and new friends were not easy to win. On the other hand, both laws and customs were decaying, and at such an alarming rate that I, who had been so eager to engage in public affairs, began to suffer from dizzy spells because I realized that I was watching the whole thing rushing towards destruction.

> It is true that I did not stop hoping for salvation. I was still hoping for a suitable moment for me to act. In the end, however, I came to the conclusion that all states existing today, however many there are,

---

[26] For a moving depiction of Scorates' last arguments, see Jacek Bocheński, *Divine Julius*, Epilogue, After Plutarch

are badly governed. Their laws are incurably sick, and some extraordinary treatment would be necessary to heal them. But to accomplish that, so many happy circumstances would have to come together! And this led me to discover the glory of philosophy. Because only from her elevated perch can you see what is right in both public and personal life. And it seems that evil will not cease to oppress the human race until...

TWO DECISIONS

I realize perfectly well that this trick is all too easy: to break an important argument mid-sentence—and just as Plato is about to reveal what he sees as the ultimate salvation for states and, therefore, for all humanity, too. Many writers use similar tricks to keep the reader interested. But I am not doing it for such a purpose. Nor am I guided by some sort of literary perversion so fashionable among modern writers. The reason is different and simple: I want to show how suddenly and unexpectedly the events of real life impinged upon the realm of my philosophical studies. For it so happened that just as I was in the middle of this section of the Seventh Letter, two momentous decisions were made in Pudentilla's house.

I will spare my readers a detailed account of how the first one came about because I have probably devoted too much space to it already. In short: I have decided to marry Pudentilla. I informed Pontianus about it, and he informed his mother. She accepted my proposal gracefully. Apparently, all my previous efforts—my spells, poems, conversations, and hints— had their effect.

But as soon as the matter was settled, Pontianus began to insist that the wedding should take place as soon as possible. Pudentilla, with my full support, raised objections:

"Pudens must put on a man's robe first, and you should find yourself a wife. I want to take on new responsibilities knowing that I have fulfilled my old ones and that my sons are now completely independent."

Pontianus circled for some time and finally said, with a very modest air, that he had already chosen a girl.

"Who is it?" asked Pudentilla.

"I'm going to marry Herennia, daughter of Rufinus," Pontianus replied with proud firmness.

We were stunned.

THE BRIDE OF PONTIANUS

We tried to dissuade Pontianus from marrying Herennia for a long time and as hard as we could, but he stubbornly persisted in his decision, deaf to all arguments—both mine and his mother's. Evidently, the girl was skilled in love and managed to befuddle his discernment completely. And yet he knew very well—I told him this myself—that Herennia had until recently entertained private visits of a young man from a leading family in Oea. I also recounted to him what Saturninus had once told me: that an astrologer had read in the charts that Rufinus' daughter would soon marry but then be quickly widowed. It turned out, however, that Pontianus remembered the teachings of our masters in the Academy as well as I did, for he replied calmly, quoting a sentence from *Timaeus*:

"Stars and planets send signs and omens to those who cannot reason!"

And how could I reply to him that, in my view, the more probable version of the text was the one omitting the negation "not"? It seemed to me absurd and even humorous to start a discussion in this African town about the correct reading of a sentence of Plato's only to dissuade a passionate young man from marrying a girl with an uncertain past.

A marriage contract was prepared. The bride solemnly arrived at the bridegroom's house. She arrived calm, almost indifferent, not blushing, for she had long since grown out of the shyness of a virgin.

The litter was carried through the streets of the city by eight porters. The witnesses of the procession will surely remember this unusual sight: on the way to her husband's house, the girl ostentatiously allowed herself to be seen and even teased young men along the way. Her cheeks were rouged and her eyes painted, and her face was seen clearly, obscured only by the thinnest of flame-colored veils.[27]

She brought her dowry in cash, that much was true. Four hundred thousand. But all that money had been borrowed the day before! It was a dowry much larger than the poverty of her large family allowed. But old Rufinus knew what he was doing. While he had no fortune, he never lacked ideas. And his appetite was good too—for Pudentillas four million. He took additional comfort in the forecasts of the astrologers. But in order for these plans to succeed, I had to be removed first. With me gone, it would be easy to corner the naive son-in-law and the lonely Pudentilla.

The old man quickly set about his work. He dressed down Pontianus at every opportunity. The servants reported to us his speeches to his son-in-law:

"What possessed you to marry your mother to this Apuleius? Have you gone mad to give your family fortune to a stranger voluntarily? What risks you are running! And all because you read some Plato together! What is the guarantee of friendship and honesty in money matters? Get out of this business before it's too late!"

And he threatened his son-in-law that if he did not get rid of me, he, Rufinus, would take his daughter away from him because he could not allow his beloved child to live with someone so irresponsible and obviously condemned to poverty. It was not difficult for him to convince the simple-minded Pontianus, while Herennia employed other means of persuasion. So, in accordance with the wishes of both, my friend went to see his mother to dissuade her from marrying me. To dissuade her from a marriage which he had most passionately urged upon us both!

---

[27] *Flammeum*: the veil worn by a Roman bride

RUFINUS'S THREATS AND PUDENTILLA'S LETTER

Pudentilla heard her son's words with her usual seriousness, but she remained unmoved. She reproached him very severely for being reckless and thoughtless. Pontianus took the reply to his father-in-law. Apparently, he excused himself to him and explained that his mother was of an unwavering character in general and did not easily change a decision once made; and now she was firm in her intention, and the demand to break with me hurt her painfully. Besides, it is well-known that anger usually gives strength to stubbornness. He reported Pudentilla's words:

"I know very well that you come to me at Rufinus's instigation. That is why I will need my husband all the more: as a defense against the brazen greed of your father-in-law."

Rufinus quivered with rage. He began to heap upon Pudentilla, a woman of impeccable and modest character, the most vile insults. And in front of her son, too! Many people witnessed the incident and repeated to us the words that were then spoken:

"Your mother is a seductress! Her lover, Apuleius, is a sorcerer and poisoner! I could strangle him with my own hands!"

Meanwhile, Pudentilla, upset by the whole affair and the unexpected change in her son's attitude, decided to leave Oea for a while. She went to her suburban property (and of course brought me along). From there, still resentful and angry, she wrote a letter to her son. She wrote it in Greek, as that was the language she spoke most freely. Here are a few significant words from that letter:

I wanted to get married for the reasons I had explained. You yourself convinced me that I should choose Apuleius rather than anyone else. You spoke of him with admiration and made every effort to ensure that he should enter our family by marrying me. Now those mean people are attacking us, and they managed to get you to change your mind. And now, suddenly, Apuleius is a magician, and I love him because I have been enslaved by his sorcery. So come to me while I'm still sane!

Of course, this last ironic sentence could be misinterpreted. However, she ended the letter with a clear statement:

"I am not a victim of witchcraft, and I am not in love. Nobody, however, can escape what is destined for him."

Pontianus, naive and credulous, did the stupidest thing possible: he not only showed the letter to his father-in-law—he gave it to him.

THE WEDDING AND THE DOWRY

Obeying his mother's wish, Pontianus came to our village with his wife. We all stayed there for two months, although the situation was rather strange and the mood was not very cheerful: we could all sense the coming storm. Pudentilla was very busy running the estate; every day, she meticulously reviewed the reports of the steward, the grooms, the shepherds. Nevertheless, she still found time and strength to remind Pontianus of his behavior and intentions at every opportunity. She rebuked him sharply and exhorted him to beware of Rufinus's plot. She especially resented the fact that he and his father-in-law had read parts of her letter to strangers in order to misrepresent it. Of course, what they read was that sentence ironically calling me a magician who had enslaved her with love magic.

Then, in that villa outside the city, our wedding took place, and our property contract was signed. It is natural for you to ask, why did we choose that secluded place? The explanation is simple. Not so long ago, Pudentilla laid out about fifty thousand sesterces for Pontianus's wedding; it was her own money, and it had all gone to gifts to the citizens of Oea who flocked to the celebrations. It was an old custom, and the loss had to be borne in the case of the oldest son. But no one can blame us for wanting to save ourselves such an expense. We also wished to avoid all those receptions and formal visits to which newlyweds are bound by custom. This, and only this, made us hold the wedding ceremony away from the city, modestly and quietly.

However, people who are less kind to us than they are disappointed in their expectation of gifts soon began to spread rumors that I was to blame for everything. It was said that I took Pudentilla to the country to have a free hand entangling her with my intrigues and magic tricks. A total falsity!

The marriage contract stipulated that Pudentilla would give me three hundred thousand sesterces as her dowry. This was one hundred thousand less than Herennia had brought. Yet Pudentilla was one of the richest women in the city and perhaps in the province. What better proof could there be that I had absolutely no intention of getting rich by marrying Pudentilla?

What's more: the dowry was not paid in cash but remained as a claim on Pudentilla's estate. An additional clause stipulated that upon her death, the dowry was to go entirely to her sons, Pontianus and Pudens, if she should die without any children by me, and if she gave birth to our child, then half of the dowry would go to it, and the other half to her two sons from her first marriage.

Wedding contracts usually don't have such provisions. No one is surprised if a widow of average beauty and slightly above middle age desiring to marry lures a suitor using a large dowry and particularly favorable financial terms, especially when it comes to a young, handsome (if I may say so), educated, and relatively wealthy man.

THE CONTRITION OF PONTIANUS

It is often said that the study of philosophy takes one away from the matters of this world, makes him helpless in matters of property, and condemns him to poverty and misery. I have never thought so and have even tried to the best of my modest ability to disprove this common view. Here I was in Oea. I had come to this city with only one slave, but my love of wisdom has greatly helped me here: it paved my way to the house of Pudentilla and later to my marriage with probably the richest woman in this part of Africa.

As I have just explained, Pudentilla brought me a very modest dowry, but at her side, I could live well; and the matter of her testament remained open. I haven't thought about it yet. At the time, it seemed important to spread the word of my generosity to my stepchildren and make sure it reached the ears of interested parties.

So, after our return to Oea, I wrote a letter to the governor of our province, Lollian Avitus, whom I knew well, in which I gave a very detailed account of my stay in Oea and my marriage with Pudentilla, portraying it all in the correct light of course. In my letter, I spared no words of regret for the conduct of Rufinus, under whose influence my unfortunate stepson Pontianus had fallen, and I left this letter, apparently unfinished, on the table in the library.

Needless to say, I did it on purpose: I was sure that someone among the servants would read it and immediately report it to Pontianus in order to inform him of the great danger: Apuleius writes to the governor himself, his friend, reporting all the domestic troubles and speaking ill of Pontianus and this can ruin the career of a young man who would like to become a lawyer.

The effect was immediate. Pontianus came to our house with his younger brother Pudens. Crying, he threw himself at his mother's feet. He begged her to forgive him for what he had done. Kissing our hands—the hands of Pudentilla and mine—he begged us to forget that he had been deceived by Rufinus and people like him. He assured us that he was even ashamed of our benevolence. Finally, he revealed what else he meant: he wanted me to write a letter to Lollian Avitus recommending him, Pontianus: his person and his abilities.

I willingly acceded to this request. All the more so that Avitus (I had learned about it confidentially) was about to leave office. So my letter of recommendation would not really achieve anything.

Pontianus, grateful and deeply moved, left for Carthage with my letter of introduction in hand. I, on the other hand, at last calm and happily married, was able to return to Plato.

I DREAM ABOUT HOLDING POWER

And so it is time for me to return to that sentence of the Seventh Letter, which I interrupted so abruptly when the matrimonial matters—mine and Pontianus's—burst onto the peaceful current of my philosophical studies. Let me remind you: Plato claims that evil will not stop oppressing the human race until... And here are the great words, constantly repeated, quoted, and commented on:

> until those who love wisdom truly and properly take power; or else, by some divine dispensation, the rulers begin to study philosophy.

Perhaps I now ought to launch on a scholarly argument in the professorial style: about the vocations of philosophers and politicians; about the unity of the highest social and individual good; and about the essence of power and wisdom. This is what I should write. But, to be honest, my first thoughts after reading Plato's words were not so lofty. I began to wonder—as a joke, of course—how this great maxim might apply to me. I thought:

Since I—so devoted to philosophy—have also turned out to be a man of prudence in business, outmaneuvering even the old hand Rufinus, I suppose I could also handle matters of state. In fact, I might even lead them more sensibly than many statesmen. After all, politics is not more difficult (contrary to popular opinion) than managing a household, family, or property and dealing with the plots and intrigues of our friends and neighbors. Whoever can maneuver well the reefs of everyday life will also sail efficiently between the Scylla and Charybdis[28] of great politics. If you think about it, the problems here and there are identical in their nature and require similar skills to solve them: a little cunning, a lot of distrust, and the ability to anticipate ordinary human reactions. You also need the ability to make the right

---

[28] Scylla and Charybdis: in Greek mythology, two immortal and irresistible monsters who beset the narrow waters traversed by Odysseus in his wanderings (Homer, *Odyssey*, Book XII). They were later localized in the Strait of Messina.

gestures at the right moments. Gestures, I repeat, not deeds!

So many rulers and leaders in different countries and epochs have come from the lower classes; they were generally uneducated and often came to rule by chance, and yet they did well. We all too easily succumb to a certain error of perspective. For standing below, we look upward at those above us; because they stand higher than us, we think they are better. And yet, they are the most ordinary of people! They handle current affairs in ways that are not always sensible, and only flatterers and the dumber among historians see in their words and deeds some wonderful depth, identifying some profound and brilliant motivation for their simplest actions. Therefore all this historiographic talk is like the hollow clattering of cymbals.

But a philosopher in power would differ from an ordinary politician in that he would not only lead the state quite well but would also have a great goal in mind: to build a new community, law-abiding, peaceful, and just. Such a man devoid of personal ambition, intellectually and ethically superior to mere mortals, would lead his people toward the haven of a happy future with a firm hand.

At that point, my meditations ceased to entertain me. Mainly because I am not quite sure to what haven I should lead a country entrusted to me.

In principle, I should have a ready answer: towards the one that my master, Plato, devised as a perfect system. But because of my recent study, I had certain details of this constitution fresh in my memory: the common possession of women; the various levels of guardians; taking children away from their parents; banishing poets; improving old works so that they can serve current needs.

I decided that the issues of demonology and current property matters were closer to my heart.

A SYSTEM WORTHY OF A PHILOSOPHER

But enough jokes. After all, I touched on a matter that was probably the greatest and most sacred for the founder of the Academy. Some of our teachers see it as central to his philosophy. They claim that it fascinated him truly and deeply. Not the universal ideas existing somewhere in a pure form, not the migrations of the soul, not the creation and functioning of the cosmos, and not even the nature of god himself, the creator of everything! We must always bear in mind (which I do, perhaps even with too much stubbornness) that Plato, from his youth until the end of his life (when he composed *The Laws* and wrote the Seventh Letter), was, above all—a politician. An unfulfilled politician, of course, as he never had the opportunity to put his ideas into practice in life—but nevertheless, one who never ceased looking for such possibilities. So perhaps I should not deflate with my untimely reflections what he regarded as the most precious of his mental constructions.

Plato reasoned as follows: since philosophers are superior in wisdom and moral standing, it is right and just that they, the most worthy of men, should guide ordinary men who left to their own devices, only blindly follow their impulses.

But just as I thought that, something made me wonder. Maybe my playful fantasizing that I, Apuleius, should have the right to claim power was not altogether misplaced? The words of Plato that either the rulers must become philosophers or philosophers—rulers are considered shocking today. But why? Because the seekers of wisdom are seen as detached from practical life, as helpless fantasists and dreamers? My example proves that it doesn't have to be that way. Yet, this opinion about philosophers was already common in Plato's time. I open the sixth book of *The Republic*, and what do I find there? This statement by Adeimantus, Plato's brother:

"He who studies philosophy too long becomes a useless freak. Even the best of philosophers are completely useless to the state."

Socrates answers this in a long and roundabout way and, to my mind, not very convincingly. First, he attacks Sophists, pseudo-pedagogues, and teachers of empty mental tricks. Finally, he comes to this conclusion:

> In a perfect state, under a perfect political system, the perfect man can come into existence. Provided, however, that some necessity compels the very few lovers of true wisdom to enter politics—all those who are generally considered not evil but—useless. Of course, another condition would have to be satisfied simultaneously: namely, that the state—the society—begins paying attention to philosophers. Then one can imagine a situation where the sons of today's rulers become admirers of wisdom and faithfully follow its instructions.

A little further on, Socrates puts it graphically:

> There are very few philosophers worthy of the name today. And they don't want to reveal themselves. For how do things stand in all the states on earth? There is no sensible government anywhere. And it would be difficult to find any government or ruler interested to improve the situation. A rational man feels as if cast among wild animals. Of course, he won't impose himself upon other people, but the truth is that he can't even oppose the bestiality around him. He will accomplish nothing and will only find an early grave. So he sits quietly and occupies himself with his own affairs.
>
> Just as it happens in winter: the wind brings clouds, dust, and rain, so a man huddles somewhere under a wall. Watching others commit all kinds of infamy, he must consider himself lucky to have kept his hands clean. This is how he will live—in hiding—until his time of departure. And that will happen with beautiful hope, quietly, and with his mind at peace.

THE RETURN FROM CARTHAGE

The last words of the previous chapter stuck in my memory forever, for no sooner had I written them down than the sad news of Pontianus reached me.

By marrying Herennia, he had succumbed to passion. Not a wholesome thing, but after all, forgivable. Plato's writings prove how vulnerable he was to the slings and arrows of Eros, both he himself and Socrates. I have already quoted a number of scenes and statements that well reflect this weakness of both men. And let me remind you of Plato's love elegies, which I recited during my first visit to Pudentilla, my present wife, or the meeting between Socrates and Charmides, Plato's uncle, and the words of the sage:

"I am no judge of beauty. I find gold in every beautiful boy, and almost all young boys seem beautiful to me."

I could point to many similar instances. They make me appear far more reserved than the two philosophers, for I took a wife after a truly philosophical reckoning. So, I cannot blame Pontianus for having fallen so suddenly and madly for that seductress Herennia, especially since he quickly regained his senses. His letters to me, written from Carthage and later, on his way back, make this clear. He left for the capital of our province to pay respects to Lollian Avitus. Thanks to my recommendation, the governor received him kindly and, as he was a well-educated man and even seriously interested in philosophy, he congratulated Pontianus on having found such a good stepfather and that he so quickly saw through Rufinus's intrigue and corrected his behavior towards me. All this boded well for the future, even if a new governor were to be appointed. Pontianus must have realized while in Carthage that such an appointment was imminent. Seeing as much, he decided to return to Oea.

The journey, which normally takes a dozen or so days, took longer than expected, and, for Pontianus, it became a journey into eternity.First, I received a letter from him, in which he warmly assured me that he saw in me his real father, master, teacher, and that he felt fine. The next letter, also full of cordiality, ended with the following note: "My health is not so good. Therefore, I will either break my journey altogether, or I will continue very slowly." Finally, a third letter arrived, short and somewhat sad, though apparently indifferent;

but it was apparent that Pontianus was preparing for the worst. The postscript was strange: "I am writing a new testament. I will designate my mother and brother as primary heirs. Herennia will receive a legacy: linen sheets worth two hundred sesterces."

What's that supposed to mean? Why this mocking legacy to his wife? After all, the wedding had taken place only a few months earlier! She certainly wasn't bored with him yet. Has she cheated on him all the same? In any case, it would have been better to omit her completely from the will. A legacy of worthless bedsheets would subject her to mockery for many years.

And then came the messenger with the news that Pontianus had died.

I MEDITATE IN THE LIBRARY

Pudentilla locked herself in her room, mourning the death of her firstborn son. I spent the whole day in the library. It was the same spacious hall in which I had placed my sacred objects modestly wrapped in linen upon my first arrival in the house. All the books were still there. They had served me well during so many months of my work on Plato. Pontianus had bought these books in Athens while we were studying together in the groves of the Academy, for back then, he was an enthusiastic lover of true wisdom.

How much I owed to this young man! He brought me across the threshold of the hospitable home of Pudentilla. He exerted himself to allow me to marry the mistress of the house. And finally, it was his library that allowed me here, in this a provincial town, to study the life and thought of Plato, thus returning to the memories of our young Athenian years.

I didn't write a single word all day. I was looking at the last lines of my last chapter:

This is how he will live in hiding until his time of departure. And that will happen with beautiful hope, quietly, and with his mind at peace.

Verily, it is in such a mood, in such undisturbed internal serenity, that every true disciple of Plato should die. Anyone who has absorbed with his heart and mind the teachings of the master which are constantly repeated and reconsidered in his dialogues:

The noblest—the thinking—part of the soul is the work of the Creator God Himself. It existed before the mortal body was formed, and after the body dies, it returns to its stellar abode, to the world of eternal beauty, whose memory, however dim and unclear, it always carries within itself. But this happy and instant return comes only to those chosen souls who have sincerely loved true wisdom. But with most souls, it is otherwise. For souls that are too much entangled with the body, loving it and yielding to its desires, and thus imbued with its mortal nature—such souls cannot detach themselves completely from the heavy, visible elements and cannot waft up into the upper air. So they stay near the ground and wander among graves, where shadows and apparitions are said to be common. But after a while, they re-enter other bodies and are reborn as living beings. The worst and most polluted souls become evil, bloodthirsty animals; thus, sadist and harsh despots may incarnate into hawks or wolves. But those who have lived honestly, although they did not know true wisdom—they start a new existence as bees or ants, or may even reside in a human body until they are completely purified by going through many subsequent incarnations and are ready to return to their heavenly homeland.

The thought is beautiful and simple. However, when it comes to considering the posthumous fate of any particular person's soul in the light of this theory, great difficulties immediately arise. Let us take the life of Pontianus as an example. When he dealt with philosophy, he did so with great zeal. He spared no time, effort, or money—as is evidenced by his library. And he wasn't just collecting any old books—because he knew the works of Plato very well, not worse than me. Yet, later he departed from philosophy: first for law and eventually for

Herennia. So what will happen to his soul? How many years shall his soul wander among graves? And with how many new incarnations—and in what kinds of bodies?—will it pay for its lack of perseverance and its inability to resist desire?

THE FUNERAL OF PONTIANUS

But now something totally unexpected happened, something nobody would have predicted.

Pudens was still living in our home. He had not yet donned the men's robe and we managed him rather strictly. His mother and I chose good and demanding teachers for him. I insisted on this because, on my first visit to this house, I noticed that Pudens really only knew Punic. He spoke Greek only insofar as he had learned it from his mother, and he could barely put a sentence together in Latin. All of this, of course, was so because he had largely kept the company of village simpletons. It's clear that my admonitions and methods could not win me the boy's friendship. If only I could have foreseen what trouble my aversion to Punic and my love of correct Latin would cause me!

We prepared Pontianus's funeral with the greatest care, observing all the usual ceremonies. The corpse was carried in a solemn procession beyond the city limits, where there was an imposing family tomb by the road leading east to Leptis Magna. There we stopped for a while to perform the last rites. None of us—lost in sorrow and mourning—noticed that Pudens had somehow disappeared. But when we returned to the city in the evening, we knocked in vain at the gate of the house: it had been locked. Pudens appeared on the roof with a group of teenagers like him and refused to open the door for us. He shouted at the top of his voice that this was his home; that he was entitled to it upon his brother's death; that Pontianus bequeathed his fortune only to him because his mother is rich anyway, but that we forged a different will; that he would not allow his mother to give his entire fortune to a stray dog named Apuleius who had possessed her with sorcery.

Crowds of neighbors flocked immediately. People were screaming, laughing, some taking one side, others another. I don't know how all this would have ended had it not been for a few stout farmhands among our servants. They climbed the roofs of a nearby house, jumped over onto our roof, and, after a fierce fight, chased the friends of Pudens away.

Pudens immediately moved out to live with his uncle, Emilianus. They had barely seen each other until then. Emilianus probably didn't even know what his nephew looked like and certainly wouldn't have recognized him in the street. Only now did the deep family sentiment revive in the two of them.

I understand Pudens. Our house regime was strict. He was forced to study. I forbade him to speak Punic and corrected almost every word of his Latin. The boy saw me only as a sour professor, a joyless bookworm, and, perhaps, a crafty sorcerer who had already taken his mother and would take all his fortune. In Emilianus's house, however, he found absolute freedom. His uncle gave him a man's robe, so he was now formally of age. Books went into the corner, and tutors were chased away. Pudens spent whole days wandering around taverns. He was always drunk and often in the company of girls of loose morals. He also visited the school of gladiators: he knew all those murderers by name.

So, I repeat, I understand Pudens. But what was Emilianus's interest in this? When people asked me about it, I made a mysterious face, spread my hands helplessly, and then deftly brought the conversation to the topic of inheritance law. I asked, as if in disbelief:

"Is it true that if Pudens were to die without leaving a will, his estate would go to his uncle?"

But my enemies did not leave that without a response. They now spread the rumor that I have helped Pontianus move on from this world. Lucky for me, he had died far away from Oea, but people whispered all the same that I had poisoned him with the help of a slave. Still others claimed that I knew spells which could cause death at a distance.

And now Rufinus and Herennia reentered the stage.

THE CASE OF A CERTAIN STATUE

One day, Pudentilla came back from the city very agitated and immediately told the girl to ask me to her chamber. Although she usually exercised exaggerated restraint in her movements and words, she now flew completely out of control and began to reproach me violently without a preamble:

"Do you know what people say about you? They say you have a skeleton statuette among your books! They say you celebrate magical rites, and the statuette obeys you like a slave. You can use it to cause the death of whomever you want. They say that's how you got rid of Pontianus! You don't have to defend yourself, don't try to convince me. I myself know very well that it is all stuff and nonsense. The same as that thing that I fell in love with you because you enslaved me with spells and love potions. But I've had enough of your secrets and of you staying locked up in the library! What are you hiding there? What is in this linen bundle on the altar of our household deities?"

I don't need to describe how terrified I became. The matter was serious and—dangerous. If I were charged with magical practices, I could lose not only Pudentilla, and not only my fortune, but even my life. I did my best not to show my wife that my heart was beating wildly. Without a word, I pointed my wife to the library door. We entered the spacious, shady, cool room, filled with the delicate scent of papyrus, so pleasant to me. On the table, a white scarf covered several objects. I didn't take it all off, but only slightly lifted one corner and pulled out the statuette.

"Here is the skeleton," I said, striving for a tone of irony.

The figurine, made of dark ebony, represented a young man with a thick, soft beard and curly hair unruly running out from under a wide-brimmed hat. Draped over his shoulders was a short coat. It was, of course, god Mercury himself. This was plainly indicated by the two tiny wings at his temples. The whole thing was made of thin ebony slats, which the master had fitted and glued so perfectly together that, had I not seen with my own eyes the box that had been broken to make those slats, I would have sworn the thing had been carved from a single piece of wood. The master craftsman was, of course, Saturninus. The ebony had been obtained by Pontianus; he had got it somehow from a certain lady, just as he had promised he would as we left the sculptor's workshop. Out of it, Saturninus first made for me the model of the cosmos. When he brought it, we had that interesting conversation about the direction of rotation of the universe. I received the statuette from him a little later, but still before my marriage to Pudentilla.

I prayed to this figurine on various holidays. I offered to it sacrifices of incense and wine and sometimes blood sacrifices, too. Someone among the servants must have seen it. But he saw inaccurately or reported maliciously, for he made of the handsome young man a grim likeness of a skeleton. Or was there another source of this lie?

Unexpectedly, as if thanks to Mercury himself, I had an illumination. As Pontianus and I were leaving Saturninus' workshop, Rufinus had barred our way in the narrow street. I jokingly told him that we had just ordered a statuette of a skeleton. Rufinus believed it, and he himself even told us something about the ring on which a headless lion standing over a supine skeleton was carved. So everything became clear. Someone, probably Pudens, told him that I was making offerings to a figure made of wood, while Rufinus concluded that the figurine was a representation of a skeleton. It seemed to follow that the two had entered into an understanding. If so, Herennia would be sure to join the alliance shortly.

And at that moment, Pudentilla, as if following the trail of my unspoken thoughts, said with a new fit of fury:

"The skeleton is fine, it's just slander, and I didn't believe it for a moment. But what I haven't told you yet hurts me a hundred times more because it is true: Rufinus wants to marry Herennia to Pudens!

Think, a brother is to marry his brother's widow! And so much older than him! I will never get over it!"

And then she added with truly feminine ruthlessness in her voice:

"Herennia is a curse on our house. I really regret that you do not have a skeleton we could use. And these other things under the scarf, can none of them help us?"

I explained that they were only symbols of initiation into the mysteries of Dionysus. She understood at once what the symbols were, and out of feminine modesty, she no longer demanded that I show them to her.

As Pudentilla left the library, I carefully wrapped the statuette of Mercury in a scarf. With sadness but also with some malice, I reflected on how low the knowledge of things divine had fallen among women, even those as well-educated as my wife. They look at Mercury and see in him only a charming young man, a messenger of gods and men, a protector of students, poets, and philosophers. And yet everyone should know that the same Mercury has from time immemorial been held in high esteem in Egypt as the god Thoth, depicted with the beak of an ibis—the lord of all secret knowledge. But why turn to Egyptian beliefs anyway? Already in Homer, Hermes— that is, Mercury—leads the souls of the dead to the underworld. And he can fetch them from there, too, at the service of anyone who knows the proper incantations.

IF I KNEW MAGICAL SPELLS

Pudentilla, of course, did not know everything. I didn't have a skeleton figurine—that much was true. Nor did I know any really effective spells, either. However, I did collect—wherever and whenever I could—formulas and prayers containing a multitude of strange words from different languages: from Egyptian and Greek, from Hebrew and Persian. I studied ancient books, I inquired among friends, and I even made contacts with certain secret societies.

But I only did it for the love of knowledge, without any thought of personal gain. And I most certainly wouldn't hurt anyone. Yes, I would gladly have summoned ghosts but only to learn from them what life was really like on the other side, in the world of the dead: whether they lived in the underworld, or among us in the air, or in a distant land beyond the Ocean, where the sun sets, or among the mountains and plains of the moon. (Because there is no consensus on this matter either among philosophers or the common men).

Or I would transform myself into another being—of course, if I knew the right spells, and even then, only briefly. For example, I could transform myself into a big fish to see the depths of the sea with my own eyes.

What an extraordinary world must lie hidden under the undulating surface of the blue expanse! Even the most daring divers do not go deeper than a few dozen feet, and this only near the shore. And even the biggest fishing nets do not go much deeper. And yet there, at the very bottom, may exist great civilizations, huge cities, powerful states—exist and flourish—created by beings whose shapes and customs are simply unimaginable. They could be some kind of monster fish, crabs or starfish, mussels or snails. After all, the sea throws up all sorts of creatures, and they have fascinated me since childhood. I collected them, walking along the shore, and also bought some interesting specimens, paying a few coppers to the fishermen and the boys who brought them to me. But all of these specimens, however astonishingly multicolored and variously shaped, say little about the life of the true depths. For these creatures are to the life of the depths like the birds of the sky are to the life on earth: a creature dwelling on one of the celestial spheres can perhaps seize accidentally an eagle or a falcon blown upwards by a storm, but it cannot see what lies below, because clouds, mists, dust, and fumes, obscure its vision. And therefore—how little such a creature knows about the richness of forms of our own existence!

And speaking of birds: I would like to transform into a bird. I would glide freely into the clouds and then sail above them. I would fly to the most distant lands, over mountains and seas, over deserts and forests. I would meet peoples about whom only rumors circulate among us. I would admire the wonders of nature. I would be free, I would conquer space! I think I'm not the only one who secretly harbors such dreams, and I readily admit that they are not very worthy of a philosopher. But I also believe that humanity will never give them up as long as birds fly swiftly overhead and we remain down here, chained to the ground.

I met a man here, in Oea, who swore that he had the recipe for turning into a bird and that he could demonstrate it to me if I paid the expenses of the procedure. His name was Quintian. He lived in the house of a certain Crassus—that same Crassus about whom Rufinus had once said that he spent several months of each year in Alexandria and was there even now. One evening we locked ourselves in this house. When night fell, Quintian, by the light of a torch, made sacrifices of various kinds of birds to a secret divinity. (Of course, he had bought them with my money). And now, as the master of ceremonies, he recited a spell over a cauldron in which he brewed a foul-smelling liquid: bird's blood mixed with strange ingredients. (I had put some denarii towards those ingredients, too). Of course, I wasn't deluding myself. I foresaw that the ointment he thus fashioned would only redden the skin, and Quintian would never grow feathers. He was undoubtedly the most ordinary of fraudsters. He had found out about my interests somehow and wanted to extract some money from me. I gladly went along because it was great fun.

Now, Quintian played the role of the magician with skill and panache, and I looked very serious, though I could hardly keep myself from laughing. I was reminded of a funny Greek story about a certain young man who wanted to become a bird but due to an accidental mistaking of ointments, took the form of a donkey.

Quintian's spell remained uncompleted. We were supposed to repeat the ceremony the following day by moonlight: only then would the ointment gain efficacy, and Quintian would fly. But, luckily for him, on the morning after that first night, Crassus returned unexpectedly to Oea. Upon entering his house, he found blackened walls and fluttering bird feathers. He swore that the apartment had been ruined. From the slave in charge, he learned that I had been there, too. So he began to spread the word throughout the city that I had performed witchcraft in his house. I quickly dropped the whole business.

WEREWOLVES

Supposedly terrifying, but in fact, rather funny tales about people transforming into animals circulate among the people. My favorite author, Petronius, pokes the funniest jokes at these amusing yarns—that same Petronius who had once been one of the favorites of Nero but then had to commit suicide on his orders. Well, one of the people in his satirical novel recalls an adventure that supposedly really happened:

> Our master went to Capua on some business. I persuaded a guest who was living with us at the time to go with me to the fifth milestone, because I still had a friend there, a girl named Melissa. The fellow was a stout soldier. We set off at night, at cock's crow. The moon was shining bright as noon. We were already walking along the road between the tombs when my companion stopped to satisfy a call of nature while I sat and counted the slabs. When I looked back, the other fellow was already naked, and his clothes were lying on the ground. My soul jumped into my nose. I froze motionless like the dead. And he—first peed all over his clothes and then suddenly turned into a wolf! Don't think I'm joking. I wouldn't lie for anything in the world! But, as I began to say, when the fellow turned into a wolf, he howled and ran off into the forest. At first, I didn't know what to do. After a while, I went over to pick up his clothes, and then I discovered that they had petrified! I nearly died of fear. I grabbed my sword and began to slash the air in all directions, and I kept this up until I reached the house of my friend. I entered white as a ghost. I was almost passed out with terror, sweat was dripping off me, and my eyes were bulging like those of a corpse.

And when I finally started to calm down, Melissa wondered that I was about at such a time of night and said:

"If you'd at least come a little earlier, you could have helped us. A wolf burst into our yard and bled all the cattle like a butcher. But he got what he deserved anyway, even though he ran away—because a servant pierced his neck with a spear."

After I heard that, I didn't sleep a wink. Once the day broke, I ran to my master's house. I went to the place where the petrified clothes lay but found nothing, only a little blood. And when I finally got home, my soldier friend was lying like an ox in bed, his neck being bandaged by a doctor. Then I realized he was a werewolf. From then on, I could no longer share bread with him. I wouldn't do that even if someone were to slaughter me!

So much for that storyteller in Petronius. You may wonder that while working on a serious work on Plato, I remember such amusing tales. Well, to my justification, I must point out that the stories about werewolves are very old and found in all countries. Also, in Greece, and in connection with an ancient religious cult, too:

In the Peloponnese, in Arcadia, there is a temple of Zeus Lycaeus, or Wolf. One of its mythical rulers killed a child as a sacrifice to him and instantly transformed into a wolf. It is said that similar incidents occurred there later whenever anyone accidentally ate some of the sacrificial flesh mixed with human flesh.[29]

Plato knew this strange legend. And he started with it when, in the eighth book of *The Republic,* he proceeded to describe how one becomes a tyrant.

---

[29] Lykaia was a secret, nocturnal rite held on the slopes of Mount Lykaion ("Wolf Mountain"). Pausanias reports that the Olympic boxing champion Damarchus of Parrhasia "turned into a wolf at the sacrifice to Zeus Lykaios, and changed back into a man again in the ninth year thereafter." (Translator's footnote).

THE TYRANT'S PATH

How does an ordinary politician, Plato asks through the mouths of Adeimantus and Socrates, become a tyrant? The answer is: like a man who, at the altar of Zeus Lycaeus, ate sacrificial meat mixed with human flesh and who, therefore, must transform into a wolf.

I'll summarize that section of the dialogue, highlighting those points which seem to me the most important.

Say there is a politician whom the people keep entrusting with office because he has done a lot of good for them. However, he is not satisfied by this because he wants all power. He now begins to eliminate his opponents, accusing them of being enemies of the people while assiduously courting his own supporters. And what does he promise his supporters? Most often, he utters demagogic slogans of total debt forgiveness and redistribution of land. And when he finally seizes real and undivided power in the state, no matter how, what will his first move be? He will organize a bodyguard; of course, this will happen with the consent of the people because they believe that this politician rules for their good but is surrounded by enemies.

At first, all governments tend to be relatively benign and understanding, and the new ruler fulfills some of his promises. He is always smiling and kind and maintains that his policies will never become tyrannical. On the other hand, from his first days in power, he makes every effort to ensure some war or at least some threat of war hangs over the state. He understands perfectly that an external threat not only strengthens his power but even makes its strengthening necessary.

It's a natural course of things that, with time, signs of opposition and even hostility against the tyrant will emerge, both from his former opponents and his closest allies. Of the latter, those with the most courage may boldly criticize certain of his moves to his face. The tyrant hears this at first impatiently, then with distaste, and finally with fear and suspicion: is there more to the opposition than meets the eye? Just in case, he eliminates the daredevils, one way or another. And once he removes someone valuable from his environment, the inevitable internal logic of events forces him to successively get rid of more and more of his associates, precisely those who represent something intellectually and morally. At his side remain only individuals devoid of any qualities, especially ethical ones: careerists, dodgers, slick and slippery operators. Thus, in a tyrannical system of government, there is a consistent process of purges of the power elite: purges of its most valuable people.

The despot thus condemns himself to living among ever more vile creatures and, at the same time, gives them power over his subjects. And all the while, he is building up his bodyguard because he can't be sure of anyone. He recruits people of foreign origin or recent slaves, thinking that they will be loyal to him in any situation because his subjects hate them. Armaments, wars, the expansion of the bodyguard, the bribing of allies—all burden the public treasury immensely, and the ruler needs to look for additional sources of income. Taxes rise, and with them, the discontentment of the population, and in response—the repressions of the tyrant, more bodyguards, more army, and therefore more taxes.

Perhaps I have enlarged on Plato's thoughts a little. On the other hand, however, I have emphasized what is probably the most interesting in them: the inevitability of "the werewolfing" of the individual by power and every government's natural degeneration into the rule of the basest, as well as the inevitability of the deepening of the gulf between the tyrant and his subjects.

TYRANTS AND POETS

Plato's whole argument seems logical and convincing. But another situation is also possible, and Plato himself knew it well:

Let's assume that the tyrannical power is held by a philosopher. He decides to take it because he realizes that the country he lives in is inevitably headed for disaster because the lawlessness and stupidity of politicians are destroying it. To heal the society, the tyrant-philosopher must, of course, rule with an iron fist. But he never for a moment loses sight of his essential purpose, which is to introduce a lasting order and justice, to establish the perfect system. Alas, in order to achieve noble intentions, tyrannical methods must sometimes be used. No one understands the frailty of human nature better than the sage. He knows perfectly well that most citizens must be treated like children because they are still intellectually and ethically immature: they can't even get along with each other. Therefore, they should be taught and punished, educated and shaped so that they develop and become independent. Of course, the philosopher doesn't act alone. He selects co-workers from people like himself. They are honest, prudent, and principled. They know the direction in which the state needs to develop, so they consistently implement the ideal of the political system, which they consider to be the highest good.

The whole concept of *The Republic*—Plato's main work—is based on this premise: the rule of the philosopher-tyrant. And in how many places is the thought expressed there, sometimes in passing or in a veiled manner, that in a perfect state, drastic measures will have to be used to shape the society properly! I have already mentioned that Plato allows the rulers to use—of course, for the benefit of the governed—such a hideous and corrupting trick as the conscious lie.

Let us assume, however, that the tyrant, as is usually the case, is a ruthless and criminal man, for whom the sole and ultimate goal of all efforts is not to perfect the political system but simply to remain in power. But even he, when he reaches the peak of his aspirations, can sometimes change. A historian would certainly be able to cite many examples of politicians who climbed to power over the corpses of their opponents but, having taken the helm of government ruled justly and even magnanimously.

Let's go further. Is it a law of nature that the tyrant always removes and destroys all worthy individuals from his entourage? There must be counterexamples. Good advisors can perhaps exercise great influence over a despot; stop his bloodthirsty tendencies; show him effective and humane methods of operation; gradually broaden his mental horizons? One of the Athenian tragedians, Euripides or Sophocles, put this thought in a short epigram:

"Even tyrants grow wise when they commune with the wise."

But here is the surprising thing. Plato quotes this phrase at least twice in his works, but both times to criticize it scathingly. He attacks this statement for the first time, and quite extensively, in his dialogue *Theages*. The second time, shorter but even sharper, he does it in the eighth book of *The Republic*. He quotes the epigram and then talks about poets, authors of such "wisdom":

"They go from city to city. They gather crowds around them. They sell their voices—beautiful, resonant, persuasive—and lead state systems toward tyranny or democracy. In return, they receive wages and honor; most, of course, receive them from tyrants, and far fewer from democracy."

Then he adds maliciously that in better political systems, such poets must fall as if they lacked breath and had no strength to climb up.

Not only here does Plato express his aversion and contempt for poets; I have already talked about that. But here, in Book Eight, it is only a digression. It is important, however, because the virulence of this attack has its reasons. Or at least I suspect it does. Because he, Plato, also went astray. He also tried to make a tyrant into a sage.

However, before I present this strange story, it behooves me, for the sake of order, to return to the events after the death of Socrates. What did Plato do?

PLATO IN MEGARA

The reader of the Seventh Letter must have the impression that immediately after the trial and death of Socrates, Plato, shocked, alienated, and deeply indignant at his countrymen, left the city and went on a long journey, almost to the ends of the Greek world. Because in that letter, immediately following a violent attack on the whole of the political life of his homeland, Plato writes:

"With these views, I came to Italy and to Sicily for the first time."

A journey to distant lands would, I believe, be understandable and justified. The disciple wants to escape as far as possible from the places connected in his mind with the painful memory of his master's death; and also from people he considers his murderers. And the choice of destination should arouse our respect for the young philosopher. Here he is, arriving in Sicily, just as the mortal battle between the Hellenes and their eternal enemies, the Carthaginians, was unfolding. Despising the rotten system and the petty politicians of his homeland, Plato rushes to get to know a state whose young ruler builds a new social order almost from scratch. His name is Dionysius.[30]

However, all such a conclusion would be completely wrong. For the Seventh Letter omits—no doubt intentionally—a long and important chapter in Plato's life: the period of ten years that elapsed between the death of Socrates and his journey to Italy and Sicily. What he did during that time is known, if only generally, from various mentions by other authors.

Immediately after the death of his teacher, Plato and a group of his friends left Athens. They did not go very far, however: only to Megara, a city bordering on Attica. The reasons for their departure were surely pain and resentment, but perhaps also a fear of prosecution.

After all, it could well have happened that someone would charge the disciples of the supposedly godless criminal, Socrates. And in such a case, Plato, a close relative of Critias and Charmides, figures generally hated by the democrats, would surely have been one of the first victims.

The refugees did not choose Megara by chance. Eucleides's

---

[30] Dionysius I or Dionysius the Elder (c. 432 – 367 BC) was a Greek tyrant of Syracuse. He conquered several cities in Sicily and southern Italy, opposed Carthage's influence in Sicily and made Syracuse the most powerful of the Western Greek colonies.

hospitable home was located there. He was an elderly man, a philosopher, one of Socrates' first friends, and he accompanied him in the last moments of his life.

THE TEACHINGS OF EUCLEIDES

The philosophical views of Eucleides were a combination of Socrates' interest in ethics and the metaphysical concepts of Parmenides, a renowned thinker from the city of Elea in Italy. And thus, Eucleides taught: there is only one Being, eternal and unchanging; it is good itself; it is called variously: God, Reason, or otherwise. The arguments with which Eucleides and his disciples supported the above theory were also not terribly original. They did not give a systematic exposition but argued by resorting to questions and answers. That is, they used dialogue, the favorite method of Socrates and the Sophists. The Euclidean school also specialized in devising logical conundrums, like:

A liar claims he is lying, and therefore, he is not lying. Or: one seed does not make a pile; neither do two, or three, or four. How many grains does it take to make a pile?

Eucleides not only lectured but he also wrote, and his works were composed in the form of dialogues.

Contact with the milieu of the Megarian philosopher could not have remained without its influence on the young man Plato. Who knows whether the idea to present his views in dialogues and using Socrates as his main interlocutor did not first come to him in Megara? Such dialogues would have been a way to pay tribute to the memory of his teacher and, at the same time, to glorify his own concepts by associating them with the fame of his name.

There will perhaps come a time when such an idea will be considered too bold and even—inappropriate. And perhaps people will then say that it is inappropriate to ascribe to a dead man words he had never said. However, in keeping with the tradition of our past, I see things differently.[31] I believe that it is right, and sometimes even necessary, to use the authority of great people who have already passed away to proclaim new truths through their mouths. I even say that it benefits both sides: it resurrects and revives the dead, it updates them, you could say, and it makes it easier for new ideas to enter the world. I suppose, moreover, that Plato was deeply convinced that his theories were a natural extension of the teachings of the master and that if Socrates had never said something in his lifetime, he surely would have ended up saying it sooner or later.

Dialogue, as a distinct literary genre, was, of course, not Eucleides's invention. Various writers active in many cities of Hellas, especially Sophists, began to introduce it earlier. By their very nature, large parts of dramatic works—tragedies and comedies—are also written in the form of a dialogue, and I have already mentioned that Plato had written tragedies in his youth, probably under the influence of Critias. However, he destroyed all these works when he got to know Socrates better. Apparently, they seemed to him trivial or even harmful because they distracted the reader from searching for true wisdom.

Now, however, his literary passions have been rekindled to serve philosophy. In my opinion, Plato's writing talent lies mainly in the fact that he so skillfully combines several different elements within one work: the realistic setting, the drama of casual conversation, and the philosophical issues. And his characters are real people, not symbolic proponents of certain ideas, as often is the case with the dialogues of other philosophers.

Many of Plato's dialogues were composed in the few years following Socrates' death. In their number, we should include *The Apology*, which is in the form of a defense speech allegedly delivered before the court by Socrates himself. Two dialogues, *Euthyphro* and *Crito*, deal with incidents related to the sage's trial and execution. The

---

[31] For the opposite view of the ancient tradition on authorship, see Bart D. Ehrman, *Forged: Writing in the Name of God, Why the Bible's Authors Are Not Who We Think They Are*, 2011, Chapters 1-2

backgrounds of others are much earlier years. One of them, *Charmides*, celebrates the memory of an uncle of Plato; I have quoted its fragments already. Another was later incorporated into a much larger work, namely *The Republic:* it depicts Socrates and Plato's brothers visiting Cephalus when night celebrations were held in Piraeus in honor of the Thracian goddess. And still, other dialogues, like *Protagoras, Gorgias,* and *Hippias,* introduce great Sophists of the day into the conversation.

This literary output is truly impressive for such a short period of time. We should remember that Plato could not devote himself exclusively to writing because he did not stay long in Megara. He returned to his homeland and was soon drafted into military service. He served in another war between Athens and Sparta. He was required to serve in several campaigns, some of them abroad, because he was of military age.

Only then did he set out on a journey, and indeed a long one, but not to the west, however, as the Seventh Letter would imply, but to the south, to Egypt. This journey is very mysterious and we do not know much about it. Some even claim that it is a legend and that Plato never visited the country on the Nile. I am of a different opinion. I believe that Plato made a sort of pilgrimage to Egypt, following in the footsteps of Pythagoras. That's why I want to go there too, to drink of the secret knowledge at its fount, where these two divine masters studied themselves.

Plato did not leave for the West until after his Egyptian pilgrimage, or about ten years after the death of Socrates.

And thus, I can now return to the thread that I had interrupted. I wrote that even Plato went astray: following the example of some poets, or perhaps simply taking too seriously his own philosophical ambitions (not to say fantasies): he decided to make a tyrant into a sage.

This happened in Sicily, where a new star of Hellas was rising.

THE CAREER OF DIONYSIUS

I have gone through all the learned books I could find in Oea, but I have not been able to determine exactly in what year Dionysius was born. It is almost certain that he was a peer of Plato or just a little older. They had been born in about the same year. Their homelands were distant from each other, but they were among the richest and most populous Hellenic cities of their time. Both men rose far above their contemporaries and achieved immortal fame, though in different ways and in different fields. One owed his fame to his brilliant writings; the other was one of the greatest men of action ever produced by the Greek nation. They met. I believe that the meeting, albeit short and seemingly fruitless, had profound consequences for Plato.

I have already said much about the political situation in Athens, which so decisively shaped the life and views of Plato. It is, therefore, appropriate to recall the dramatic events that took place in Sicily because only against their background can we understand the career and activities of Dionysius. I have noticed, moreover, that even many scholars and experts in history have a rather vague notion about the history of Sicily in this period, although it had no less impact on the fate of our world than the contemporary events in Greece proper. I sometimes wonder to what some countries and events owe their privileged place in human memory, and I conclude that school textbooks and literary works determine this. Sicily and Dionysius have had poor luck with them.

The Greek cities on that beautiful and rich island, located mostly in the west and south, had been at war with the Carthaginians for centuries. And the Carthaginians had their centers mainly in the western and northern parts of Sicily. In the first year of the 75th Olympiad [480 BC], the Sicilian Greeks won a brilliant victory on the banks of River Himera; and it happened exactly in the same year in which Xerxes' forces surrounded and crushed the heroic Spartans of Leonidas at the pass of Thermopylae, and a little later Greek ships routed the Persian fleet near the shores of Salamis.

Following the Battle of Himera, peace reigned on Sicily for seventy years. A new struggle began only in the last year of the 92nd Olympiad [409 BC]. This time, the Carthaginians were the winning side. They captured and destroyed the city of Selinunt on the southern coast of the island; the ruins of its huge temples testify to its once great wealth. Sixteen thousand people were slaughtered by the victors, and five thousand were taken to Africa as slaves. A similar fate befell the city of Himera on the northern shore.

Syracuse was the wealthiest Greek city on Sicily. On both occasions, the city's democratic government tried to come to the aid of those in distress. However, the relief for Selinunt was sent too late, and that for Himera was too small and under an incompetent commander.

In the spring of the third year of the 93rd Olympiad [406 BC], a great Carthaginian army attacked Acragas. But this time, Greeks from other cities arrived in time. Thirty thousand men under the command of the Syracusan strategist Daphneus managed to break through to the besieged city. However, the Carthaginian army was still standing in its fortified camp. After eight months, the city ran out of food. The Greeks decided to abandon it. At the end of the year, the Carthaginians took the deserted city of Acragas without a fight; they didn't destroy it: they decided to use it as their winter quarters.

The news of the capitulation of Acragas shocked the Greek part of Sicily. Thousands of people moved to Syracuse, while others sent their families as far away as Italy. There was a stir in Syracuse itself, for some suspected that the Carthaginians had bribed Syracusan commanders.

During the deliberations of the people's assembly, a young officer, Dionysius, dared to make this accusation publically. He had fought at Acragas bravely, and this gained him great popularity. In his accusation, he had the tacit support of two eminent politicians, Hipparinos and Philistus, who hoped to use him to remove their rivals from power. The incredibly bold attacks that Dionysius publicly launched against the most important personalities of the state gained all the more fervent applause because the existing government, although democratic, represented largely the interests of the wealthy.

Dionysius himself came from a moderately wealthy family, but he acted as a tribune for the poorest masses. Presenting himself as a simple man, he attacked great lords who selfishly thought only of their own possessions and privileges and were ready to sell their homeland to their mortal enemies.

The government fell. Dionysius was elected to the new board of *strategoi*. Naturally.

STRATEGOS-AUTOCRATOR

After they took Acragas, the Carthaginians' next target had to be Gela, the last major Greek city on the southern coast of Sicily. There were already some Syracusan troops there, but the inhabitants now asked for food. Dionysius brought it. Once on the spot, he realized that, despite the Carthaginian threat, a sharp political struggle was unfolding in Gela between the rich and the poor. He immediately took the side of the poor. Because of him, many rich people were sentenced to death and their property was confiscated. Dionysius used the money thus raised to increase the pay of his soldiers. By doing this, he gained their total devotion; but he was praised just as fervently by radical democrats, both in Gela and in Syracuse itself. Thus, Dionysius strengthened his influence by fomenting internal strife in Greek cities—and this in the face of mortal danger from without.

Upon returning to Syracuse, Dionysius announced that he would resign his office because, he said, he could not share it with "traitors who take Carthaginian money." He knew it well because the Carthaginian commander offered him a great sum, too—and that only to remain passive.

The majority of the people's assembly showed complete confidence in the man—a man who favored the poor, hated the rich, and was brave in the field. In any case—even the moderate party recognized that a wartime situation required a unified command, that is to say, that one person should direct all affairs of the state and the army. So the other *strategoi* were deposed and, to make their departure easier, they were released from all accountability for their performance. Dionysius was hailed *strategos-autocrator*—or as we would say today— a dictator, and... again, he increased the pay of his soldiers.

Shortly afterward, Dionysius, while staying overnight in the military camp near Leontinoi, faked an assassination attempt against himself, and in a primitive way, too: some screams were heard at night near his headquarters, he took refuge in the castle and ordered fires to be burnt on its walls all night. Silly or not, the event had serious consequences: the *strategos* demanded that the people's assembly allow him to set up a personal bodyguard.[32] When this proposal was passed, he selected his guard from among the poorest people and then reinforced it with foreign mercenaries. And then, at the head of more than two and a half thousand men, he captured the main points of Syracuse, above all, the armory. Only then did he become the sole ruler of Syracuse. Now, the most influential leaders of the opposition were sentenced to death by the popular assembly, and the sentence was carried out immediately.

Bearing in mind Plato's description of a politician's road to tyrannical power, I cannot help but get the impression that among the real examples from which the philosopher derived his theory, the story of Dionysius stood prominent.

A COUP, A PLAGUE, AND PEACE

In the summer of the last year of the 93rd Olympiad [405 BC], the Carthaginians moved to besiege Gela. Dionysius hurried to its rescue but was repulsed. And while he managed to shield the retreat of the civilian population fleeing from Gela and from the neighboring

---

[32] The request that the assembly grant Dionysius the right to keep a personal body guard is an exact copy of Pisistratus (600-527 BC) and shows that legislative bodies should maintain historian-consultants to review and vet their work. (Translator's note).

Kamarina, the entire southern coast of the island now fell into the hands of the Carthaginians. Now they could strike directly at Syracuse.

Dionysius' failures emboldened his enemies; they were mainly the wealthy. They believed that in this situation, it would be possible to overthrow the autocrat because the disaffected masses of the population would turn away from him in the same way as they previously left other defeated leaders. Thus, during the retreat from Camarina, the cavalry—composed almost entirely of the sons of the wealthy—rushed ahead of the rest of the army and entered Syracuse. They robbed the house of Dionysius and raped and tortured his young wife so horribly that she soon died. Or perhaps she committed suicide. And having done so, the heroes peacefully dispersed to their homes, convinced that the tyrant had been dealt with.

But the foot soldiers, made up of the levies of the poor, remained faithful to Dionysius. At their head, he hurried after the cavalry as fast as he could and entered the city a few hours after them, at midnight. The city was easily cleared of insurgents, and those unable to escape in time were slaughtered. And in this way, because of the failed rebellion, the power of the tyrant who professed to be the spokesman and protector of the common people was further strengthened. By now, all his opponents have been removed.

Happily for Dionysius, the Carthaginian threat soon passed. A pestilence had broken out in the enemy army; it had already begun at the time of the siege of Acragas, and now it raged with particular intensity. As things stood, the Carthaginians could not possibly undertake any offensive action. The cold and rainy winter was approaching.

Good news also came from Sparta, which had traditionally favored Syracuse.[33] Lacedaemon could now send men and ships because the long war with Athens was just about over: the Spartans had seized most of the Athenian warships in the Hellespont and were preparing to besiege Athens itself. (I have mentioned here that this

---

[33] Like Spartans, Syracusans were Dorians. (Carthage had been founded by Corinth).

siege was to end after a dozen or so months with the capitulation of
the city, the overthrow of democracy, and the introduction of the rule
of the Commission of Thirty headed by Critias).

The Carthaginians, well aware of the current situation, were
the first to offer peace. Though the conditions were not very favorable
to the Greeks—all the cities which the Carthaginians had captured
were to remain in their possession—Dionysius had no choice. It was
agreed that the Greek population could return to the captured cities
and live and work there in peace as free men, but paying tribute to their
new masters.

THE GOVERNMENT OF DIONYSIUS

The Commission of Thirty, which came to power in Athens at the end
of the Peloponnesian War, sought support among the wealthy and
persecuted democrats. At the same time, in Syracuse, the greatest city
of the Greek West, a soldier took power, and that, too, happened as a
result of the disasters of war. Yet there, the *strategos-autocrator* sought
support among the poor and persecuted the wealthy. And thus, in
both countries, similar, tyrannical systems of government arose, except
that in one of them, the regime turned against the wealthy, and in the
other—against the poor. But the forms of repression and lawlessness
were the same.

Critias was unable to achieve what Dionysius did. Perhaps
because, as an older man, he lacked the energy and the perseverance of
a young soldier—for he certainly did not lack the intention or the
ruthlessness. Also, Critias was not alone; he was hampered by the
presence of the Commission of Thirty, in which not all agreed as to the
goals or methods, but all had great ambitions and all intrigued against
each other. And one more thing: in Athens, the attachment to the
democratic form of government was very strong, and tyranny had
been hated for generations.

After less than a year in power, the Commission of Thirty was overthrown, and the old democratic system was restored. Yet, at the same time in Syracuse, Dionysius, though he faced great dangers, emerged victorious from all trials and consolidated his power.

Immediately after making peace with Carthage, the *strategos-autocrator* carried out radical social and economic reforms. He confiscated the possessions of the wealthy, and he could do it all the more easily because almost all his opponents had left Syracuse, settling in the town of Etna, located on the slopes of the volcano. Dionysius parcelled out their agricultural land among the landless and his soldiers, and even slaves, to whom he gave both freedom and citizenship. Likewise, he redistributed the houses of his enemies. In this way, he tied to himself many thousands of people who owed everything to him and who, in the event of his defeat, would lose everything.

But the tyrant was cautious. He knew how changeable the moods and sympathies of the people were. So he also took care of more specific ways to secure his rule. The old town of Syracuse lay on a peninsula called Ortygia. On the order of Dionysius, all the previous inhabitants had to leave it: henceforth, only his soldiers and his friends could live there. And, on the isthmus connecting Ortygia with the mainland and the new city, the ruler erected a mighty fortress which he garrisoned with his men. The fortress guarded the shipyard and one of the two ports.

A REVOLT

Trusting in the durability of the new political system, Dionysius led his troops deep into the island against a certain town which refused to recognize the supremacy of Syracuse. During the siege, however, his men mutinied. Some of the soldiers rose up against the autocrat—the rebels probably feared that he, the protector of the poor, might begin to seize their property, too. Dionysius quickly returned to Syracuse with his loyal troops. He was besieged, and his situation grew more dangerous by the day because the insurgents were soon joined by the exiles from Etna. Later they brought reinforcements from other lands and cities and even from Corinth.

After a few months, the tyrant, seeing no other hope, started negotiations. Seeing this, the besieging force neglected the most basic precautionary measures, and some of them even returned home. Meanwhile, Dionysius managed to recruit mercenaries and launched an unexpected sortie. He took one of the camps of the insurgents and forced a general retreat. But he acted magnanimously: he did not allow his men to pursue and slaughter those fleeing, and he buried the bodies of the fallen with all proper ceremonies.

This beautiful gesture paid off handsomely. The insurgents, whose army completely fell apart, agreed to Sparta's mediation, and a settlement followed. Dionysius granted pardons to all, and most of the rebels returned to Syracuse. The intransigents held out for some time on Mount Etna, but eventually, they were driven out and scattered.

All this happened in the second year of the 94th Olympiad [403 BC]. Thus, by a strange coincidence, similar political events took place simultaneously in Athens and Syracuse: civil war, fighting in the streets, and protracted negotiations with the mediation of Lacedaemon. However, in Syracuse, the tyrant, not the insurgents, was the ultimate victor.

Nevertheless, it must be said that Dionysius was careful to maintain at least the appearance of legality. The legal basis for his power was always a resolution of the people's assembly; thanks to it, as a *strategos-autokrator*, he held the important office of commander-in-chief and conducted all foreign policy; he also presided over assemblies and could levy extraordinary taxes for war purposes. However, the old institutions of government, the council, and the assembly, continued to function, even if they passed all resolutions unanimously and according to the will and recommendation of Dionysius.

THE WAR RENEWED

Within several years, Dionysius regained power beyond Syracuse. He seized several coastal Greek cities and forced the indigenous people of the island's interior, the Sicels, to recognize his suzerainty. And he was constantly building up the military. The whole of Syracuse became one great armorer's workshop. Weapons were forged even in temples. Two hundred warships were built in the shipyards, and huge fortifications were erected on the outskirts of the city.

I recall here what I had said earlier when summarizing Plato's arguments about the nature of tyranny:

From the very beginning of his reign, the tyrant has made every effort to make sure of a constant threat of external war because he understood perfectly that an external threat not only strengthened his power but even made it necessary.

In the spring of 398 BC, the people's assembly accepted Dionysius's resolution to revive hostilities with Carthage unless it voluntarily surrendered the Greek cities it had recently captured. Everyone on Sicily welcomed this resolution as the first salvo of the final reckoning. In many cities, bloody pogroms of Carthaginian merchants took place.

The plague had continued to rage in Africa for years and did not allow the Carthaginians to prepare for war in time. By the time they assembled their mercenary troops, Dionysius had captured most of Sicily. Only a few cities in the west of the island, where only Carthaginians lived, resisted him. However, the following year the situation changed radically as the Carthaginians went on the offensive. Their armies marched along the northern shore, capturing and sacking all cities along the way: even Messana fell. The decisive naval battle took place at Catana, off the eastern coast. Their advantage in the number of ships gave victory to the Carthaginians. Dionysius had to retreat to Syracuse, and the enemy proceeded to lay siege to the city by land and sea.

And now defeat hung over Syracuse. Such a defeat would have

momentous consequences for all the Greeks of Sicily and the entire West. Fortunately, many Greek states understood this in time and sent men and ships. The Greek cities of Italy especially distinguished themselves, as well as did Lacedaemon and Corinth. In the summer of 396, part of the Carthaginian fleet was routed, and the land army—camped near some marshes—again fell victim to an epidemic. Dionysios led a sortie. A part of the Carthaginian fortifications was captured, and some ships anchored near the shore were set on fire. On the fourth night after this defeat, the Carthaginian commander abandoned the battlefield: he left the port with his forty ships. But the ships carried only Carthaginians: his foreign mercenaries had to surrender to Dionysius.

And thus, Dionysius again became master of most of the island.

THE WIVES OF DIONYSIUS

As I have already mentioned, soon after the *strategos-autocrator* took power, his cavalrymen attempted a *coup d'état*. They dragged Dionysius' wife out of the house, beat her, and raped her. Soon afterward, the young woman died, possibly by her own hand. For a few years, Dionysius lived alone. But when he remarried, he married two women at once.

One of them, named Doris, came from the town of Lokroi in southern Italy; while the other, Aristomache, was a Syracusan, the daughter of one of Dionysios' closest associates, Hipparinus. The girls had been chosen mainly for political reasons: the tyrant was very keen on good relations with Greek cities in Italy, and Aristomache's family was one of the most influential in Syracuse.

The ruler of Syracuse sent a ship decorated with gold and silver to fetch his bride from Lokroi. Aristomache was brought from the city to the castle by a chariot drawn by four white horses. Both weddings took place on the same day; splendid feasts were given for the soldiers and for distinguished citizens. As contemporaries note, no one has been able to determine which one of the tyrant's wives he invited to bed first. Later, they worked out this practice: the two wives would dine at the same table with their husband, and at night, they took turns going to bed with him. All this was contrary to the usage and custom of Greeks, who had always practiced monogamy. The tyrant, of course, stood above the common usage.

The Syracusans, of course, favored their countrywoman. Meanwhile, Doris gave her husband a son; he was named after his father: Dionysius. Aristomache, although she enjoyed her husband's special affection, was unable to conceive for many years. There was a suspicion that either witchcraft or poison was the cause. Dionysius blamed the mother of Doris for the situation, and he had her murdered. Almost immediately, Aristomache gave birth to two sons and two daughters.

When Aristomache's father, Hipparinos, died, Dionysius took care of his wife's many siblings. It was then that his young brother-in-law, Dion, entered his entourage. The boy was very handsome, intelligent, and had wide interests. And the tyrant showed him great favor.

PLATO'S LIFE IN THE WEST

It's time to return to the Seventh Letter. In it, Plato states that all countries are badly ruled because their laws are incurably sick; and he comes to the conclusion that misfortune will never stop oppressing humanity until either philosophers come to power or rulers become philosophers. He continues:

"And holding these views, I went to Italy and Sicily for the first time. But the life of the West, though it is held by many to be happy, did not agree with me. All this stuffing yourself with food twice a day; all this socializing every night; and all the rest of it. Such customs will never make anyone wise, certainly, no one who has lived like this since adolescence. For what inborn virtues, however brilliant, can survive such a test? Living like this, no one ever needs to become wise! The same applies to other spiritual values.

"No country will know peace, whatever may be its system if its people think that all resources should be spent on luxuries and excesses and idleness—except, of course, the hardships of games, drunkenness, and sex. It is inevitable that states whose inhabitants live like this must constantly change their political system: now tyrannical, now oligarchic, now democratic.

"Such thoughts were on my mind when I arrived in Syracuse. I may have arrived there by accident, but I prefer to think that some higher power had taken me there."

All these words sound foreign to me, empty, and unconvincing, even if their author is the founder of the Academy. But I think I understand Plato's state of mind.

First of all, he was accustomed to the poverty of Greece proper, where even the wealthiest cities could not aspire to the riches of the West. Both Italy and Sicily are not only more prosperous but also more free, especially when it comes to matters of love. The settlers who arrived there from their mother cities cast away their conventions and old-fashioned customs: they lived here more carefree, and they reached more naturally for every delight.

I also think that Plato, like many other Athenian aristocrats, had a certain cult for the ideals of the Spartan upbringing. I don't have to elaborate what those ideals were because their fame will probably never die. Discipline, blind obedience, military service, the destruction of all manifestations of individualism will certainly have their admirers in all ages, and they shall consider them the foundation of all social health. Others, including me, cannot think about the Spartan model without a shudder of profound aversion. I understand that if this ideal of a society composed of robust and dull individuals is realized anywhere, it spells the death of all culture—just as all culture once died in historical Sparta.

Third, it was only in Italy that Plato came into direct contact with the semi-secret brotherhood of the Pythagoreans. Their teachings greatly influenced him, perhaps as much as Socrates. And Pythagoreans led an ascetic lifestyle, avoiding meat, dressing modestly, giving up their possessions for the sake of the community. So the contrast between their simplicity and sobriety on the one hand and the luxury and promiscuity of the cities of the West must have been striking for Plato.

PLATO AND DION

Why did Plato come to Syracuse? For later historians, the matter was simple: young Dion, or perhaps even the tyrant Dionysius himself, as soon as he learned that such a famous philosopher had come to Italy, immediately invited him to come. However, these historians, looking from a distant perspective, did not take into account that Plato's name was not yet very well known at that time. Although he was almost forty and an author of several philosophical works in the form of dialogues, only a relatively small group of thinkers, dispersed throughout various cities of Hellas, knew about him. Nevertheless, the claim that it was Dionysius who invited Plato is not entirely implausible. For, as I shall soon show, the tyrant, though absorbed in great political and military matters, was keenly interested in literature, willingly hosted writers, and even tried his hand at poetry.

I read somewhere that Plato went to Sicily mainly to see with his own eyes the famous volcano Etna and to investigate the causes of its eruptions (for Vesuvius was dormant then). And as he settled at the foot of the dangerous mountain, an urgent invitation came from Syracuse, which it would have been awkward to refuse. The matter cannot be resolved today, for Plato himself is very vague about the immediate reasons for his arrival in the capital of Sicily. He only says:

"I may have arrived there by chance."

We do know, however, that once he arrived there, he formed a lively acquaintance—perhaps even a friendship—with the young, barely twenty-year-old Dion. The brother-in-law and charge of the tyrant was then exactly as old as Plato had been when he had fallen under the spell of Socrates. And just as young Plato once had done, Dion, too, resolved with all the enthusiasm of youth to acquire wisdom for the good of the state and society. So it's no wonder that Plato writes about him in his Seventh Letter with great warmth:

> What do I mean that everything started with my arrival in Sicily? When I was with Dion, then still a young man; when I showed him in our conversations what would be best for the people; and when I advised him how to put it into practice... I suppose I did not realize that I was already working to abolish tyranny. For Dion was very quick and, at that time, especially susceptible to my arguments. He absorbed them as keenly and quickly as none of the young people I had ever met. He also decided to live differently than most Italians and Sicilians. He loved virtue above pleasure and luxury.

Thus, Plato's friendship with Dion is well-attested. But did Plato meet Dionysius, too? We do not find a word about that in the Seventh Letter. But it seems to me that we can take it for granted that some sort of personal contact between the philosopher and the ruler of Syracuse had taken place, for the tyrant always sought out contact with artists and writers.

THE TYRANT'S DAUGHTERS

Dionysius had given his daughters unusual names: *Arete*, or Virtue, *Dikaiosyne*, or Justice, and *Sophrosyne*, or Prudence. Of course, he chose those names not by chance but with a deeper forethought. He wanted to show to his people—and the whole Greek world—what spiritual values he considered the most precious and what goals he set for his rule.

However, something else immediately strikes me, a student of the Academy: Plato's dialogues concern themselves mainly and above all with the nature of virtue, justice, and prudence and the ways to achieve these qualities. However, it would be a mistake to assume that

Dionysius named his daughters under the influence of Plato's works because those works were just being created, or at least they were not yet known in Sicily. Therefore, another explanation comes to mind.

It seems to me that the questions of true virtue, justice, and prudence were widely discussed in those days. Not only in Athens and not only in Syracuse but in all Hellenic cities. They were, so to speak, among the leading themes of that era. Greek cities wanted brave, good citizens; they longed for just rule; they sought thoughtful leaders. It was believed that it was enough to define these concepts properly and then, through persuasion and education, instill them in everyone and thus create a perfect state.

Was this view naive? Probably. But I suspect that people of every era are somewhat naïve in this regard, for they believe deeply and unwaveringly that they will attain the fullness of happiness if only they can put into practice some abstract notion. That is why they endlessly debate their essence, argue about the correctness of terms, and give ever-new recipes for putting them into practice. And more! They are ready to die—and kill—to prove the truth of one or another combination of words; because, after all, what are definitions but combinations of words?[34]

Perhaps I am a victim of my own imagination. Rich and restless, it makes me delve into the arcane practices of magicians, now to look ahead and wonder what life will be like in ten, fifteen, twenty centuries, now to look back into the times of antiquity. And as I do that, I become quite certain of one thing—for I have learned it both by the study of philosophy and by the careful observation of the events of everyday life—mortal beings will always be just as gullible as they are now. I am neither a soothsayer nor a prophet, and thus I cannot guess the names of the idols of future generations. But I know they will exist. After all, almost any beautifully sounding word can be made into a slogan; and slogans may concern religious, social, or political life. There will always be philosophers, both very learned and foolishly arguing about the true meaning of those slogans, and fanatics who will

---

[34] Various abstract terms of Marxist ideology come to mind

love to murder each other simply because of minute differences in the definition of concepts.

If I, Apuleius of Madauros, were somehow transported into the future, what could I say to that posterity, supposedly distant, but in fact so close? I guess I would say to them this:

"Come to your senses, friends! Do not repeat the mistakes of the past. We have gone through all this ourselves—even if our words had been a little different."

And in the days of Plato and Dionysius they were different: *arete, dikayosyne, sophrosyne.*

But back to my story. In my opinion, this idea with the names of the daughters speaks well of the talents of the tyrant. He clearly understood that nothing makes government easier than the skillful use of certain words and gestures. The masses are easy to please and easy to deceive. How should they not love a ruler who is the virtuous father of Justice and Prudence?

THE TYRANT AND LITERATURE

But I wanted to talk about Dionysius' attitude to artists, and instead, I got sidetracked from the topic by discussing the names of his daughters. And yet, look: this digression has led me back to the heart of the matter. For I have just written that Dionysius wished to be known as the father of Justice; but that very same man has left us the saying that tyranny is the mother of injustice: the line comes from one of his many dramas.

Yes, you read that right: the *strategos-autocrator* wrote dramas and composed music. It is true that some have criticized his poetry, mainly because of its artificial style, full of complicated words and phrases. I cannot judge it, because if Dionysius' writings have been preserved anywhere, they can only be at the Alexandrian library. (Which is another reason to finally go to Egypt!) But here and there, one does come across some lines from his works quoted by other authors, like this line about tyranny being the parent of injustice.

Some writers quoting this line are indignant at the unprecedented cynicism of a man who publicly stated what he thought about the nature and effects of his rule. But in my view, that conclusion is probably too hasty. I suspect that in the drama, the line was spoken by one person only to be countered by another, and it probably said nothing about Dionysius' opinion regarding his rule. He may not even have considered himself a tyrant. Perhaps he justified his position to himself by arguing that during the ten years of mortal danger, someone had to take the government with a firm hand to exercise it virtuously, honestly, and prudently.

Dionysius was not only a writer himself, but he also supported artists and thinkers. One of his closest advisers was Philistus, who later became famous as a great historian. Could it be that the tyrant was also interested in literary and historical talents because he understood that, in the final analysis, posterity passes judgment on each ruler and epoch on the basis of the image created by historians and writers?

The poet Philoxenos was already famous when he was invited to the Syracusan court from the island of Cythera. He composed choral songs called dithyrambs. This genre of poetry was flourishing and evolving: music took precedence over the text, and the language became very refined. For a long time, Philoxenos enjoyed the favor of the ruler of Syracuse, but shortly before Plato's arrival, a sharp quarrel arose between them. We don't know what the quarrel was about because various authors write about it in various ways.

According to one version, the story went like this:

During a feast, the tyrant read a passage from his latest work and asked Philoxenus what he thought of it. The poet answered honestly that he did not think of it highly. The offended Dionysius forgot that he was the host and exclaimed: "You slight me because you are jealous!"

This developed into a sharper exchange, which ended, as is customary in a tyrannical state, with the order to send Philoxenus down to the quarries. But the next day, the tyrant's wrath passed, and the pardoned poet showed up at dinner. Wine was served. Dionysius, as usual, began to recite fragments of his own poems. He asked the visitor:

"What do you think about these poems?"

The poet did not reply. Instead, he stood up, beckoned to the guard, and said:

"Take me back to the quarry."

The tyrant laughed and let the matter pass. But friends warned the poet that he should not take things too far. So he promised that he would express his opinion in a way that would not deviate from the truth but, at the same time, not hurt the self-love of Dionysius.

And when, sometime later, the ruler presented his composition about some mournful events, Philoxenos decreed:

"These poems are truly pitiful."

THE SWORD OF DAMOCLES

In the end, however, Philoxenos could consider himself lucky, for he was allowed to leave Syracuse. He went to Athens, and there staged a satirical drama about a Cyclops in love with the nymph Galatea. It was widely suspected that the poet used it to mock the tyrant of Syracuse under the guise of the one-eyed giant. It was even rumored that Dionysius and Philoxenos had been vying for the attention of a girl named Galatea, and this was the cause of their feud.

A worse fate befell another artist who had spent much time at the Syracusan court. I am thinking about Antiphon, the Athenian playwright. Initially, he prospered, and many said that he made more than a passing contribution to the tyrant's dramas. Then, however, he offended his master. Allegedly, the cause was just a casual remark he made:

There was a conversation about different types of bronze and their quality. Antiphon's opinion on this matter was very definite:

"The best bronze? Why, of course, the one from which the

statue of Harmodios and Aristogeiton in Athens is made."

I think I do not need to explain to you that these two men, the killers of the tyrant Hipparchus, have been regarded for generations as the symbolic liberators of Athens. So the statement was unambiguous, and Dionysius understood it well. Antiphon paid with his life for this poetic metaphor.

One might think this anecdote was invented to blacken the image of the tyrant. However, the story could be true: Dionysius lived in constant fear. Day and night, he feared an attempt on his life. He saw conspiracies against his authority everywhere about him. He trusted no one. We know that he dismissed his barber, for the sight of the razor in his hand made him tremble. His daughters shaved him afterward. Later, however, he lost confidence even in them—Virtue, Justice, and Prudence. He took the razor out of their hands and ordered them to singe off his hair with red-hot shells of acorns instead. It was also reported that whenever he went to bed with one of his wives, he first carefully examined the passage. And the bed itself was a separate building, separated from the rest of the room by a deep moat and connected to it with a drawbridge. Dionysius raised it, locked the door of the bed chamber with a key, and only then, protected from the whole world, freely and safely indulged in the pleasures of love.

The tyrant's favorite game was football, but he couldn't play it because in order to do so, he would have to unstrap his sword. At first, he allowed himself to do it and entrusted his sword to his favorite, a young boy. However, it happened once that one of his friends said at the moment when the sword was handed over:

"You're placing your life in the boy's hands!"

And the boy laughed.

And that was enough: both men were executed. One for pointing out a possible way to kill the tyrant, and the other—for smiling at the idea.

The sword of Damocles has become proverbial. The flatterer Damocles, who praised the tyrant for his power, riches, and magnificence, went so far as to say: "There has never been anyone happier than you!" and—received an invitation to dinner. He was offered a seat on a gilded sofa covered with a beautifully woven brocade; all the crockery was of gold and silver, the dishes were most exquisite, and served by pretty boys who obeyed his every command; the scent of flowers mingled with the scent of the most precious perfumes. But no sooner had Damocles stretched himself out on his couch with contentment, but he saw with horror that a heavy, sharp sword hung directly above his neck, swaying slightly on a thin horsehair.

I have noted that the term "the sword of Damocles" is very commonly used these days to depict the horror of a mortal danger that threatens someone constantly and at any moment. Most often, however, it is forgotten that Dionysius wanted to illustrate by this gesture his own situation and thus the position of the tyrant.

I am not at all surprised that a man who was constantly afraid of the blow of the sword or the point of the dagger should punish so ruthlessly even the most indirect and allusive attacks against the essence of tyrannical power.

PLATO AND DIONYSIUS

It was with such a man and with such a situation that Plato met in Syracuse. I do not doubt that he met the tyrant in person. After all, he was not the first philosopher at his court. It seems that Aristippus, also a student of Socrates, had been there before. (His views were peculiar: he despised conventions and valued simplicity and naturalness above all else. Cheerful, witty, and sociable, he felt good everywhere and managed not to offend the tyrant).

I imagine that Plato's conversation with Dionysius had as its starting point the names of the tyrant's daughters. I imagine that the philosopher praised the idea and then, in Socratic fashion, began to wonder what these names and concepts actually meant. My supposition has some basis. According to one account, albeit late, in one of their conversations, the term *arete*, or virtue, was discussed—and that was the name of one of the daughters. At one point, Plato is said to have stated that a tyrant cannot truly possess this quality. He went on to argue that a just life is blissful and an unjust life miserable and worthy of pity—and Dikaiosyne, or Justice, was the name of the second daughter. The autocrat, the report says, understood these words as an indictment of his rule. He was also annoyed that the audience listened to Plato with such admiration. Finally, he asked him why he had come to Sicily. Plato replied that he was looking for an honest man, to which the tyrant replied with a contemptuous smile:

"You will not find him anywhere!"

Young Dion was present at the meeting. He was convinced that through these words, the tyrant gave a hint of his displeasure. Forewarned, Plato decided to return to his homeland as quickly as possible. He ended up on a ship which also carried the Lacedaemonian envoy, Pollis.

There is also another account of the meeting between the philosopher and the autocrat. The conversation was supposed to concern the essence of autocracy. Plato defended the view that in political activity, one should put in the first place not what is beneficial but what is morally right. This led to a sharp exchange of words.

Both accounts are, in my opinion, banal and unconvincing. They give the impression of literary fiction—or even a school essay on the subject: "Describe a conversation between a philosopher and a tyrant." Such essays have been written since the beginning of our civilization and will continue to be written until its last day. However, I stand by what I said before that the pretext for the main topic of conversation was most likely the names of the tyrant's daughters.

The examples I have cited, and especially the fate of Antiphon, make it seem likely that Dionysius—a suspicious man and quick to anger—felt offended by some careless word of Plato. But I think something else really annoyed him, namely the passionate friendship that suddenly and spontaneously sprang up between young Dion and the Athenian philosopher. Plato himself tells us in his Seventh Letter that Dion was eager to learn and especially open to his ideas. He understood them quickly and decided to change the ways and goals of his life altogether. Of course, we do not know the specific content of Plato's teachings. But the words of the Seventh Letter are very significant here: "I don't think I realized at the time that I was already working in some way to overthrow tyranny."

Had I been in Dionysius's place, I would have killed, or at least banished, this visitor from Athens immediately—a beautiful spirit and a corrupter of youth.

PLATO ENSLAVED

Though they differ on details, almost all the ancient authors agree that on his way back from Syracuse to Athens, Plato had an unpleasant adventure: he was sold into slavery. This was the doing of the Lacedaemonian envoy Pollis: he captured Plato and handed him over to slave traders when their ship touched the shore of Aegina. This island lies between Attica and the Peloponnese; its hills can be clearly seen from Athens with the naked eye, so Plato lost his freedom practically at the gates of his homeland. Athens and Aegina had fought bloody wars with each other for centuries, and therefore the inhabitants of the island had traditionally been friends of Lacedaemon; and in those years, a Lacedaemonian navy was based there. No wonder Pollis could be so bold.

Of course, the envoy did this at Dionysios' behest. Some even say that the tyrant had asked Pollis to kill Plato while they were still at sea, if at all possible, but sell him into slavery if not. That should have been no hardship for him, said the tyrant: on the contrary, as a just man and a lover of wisdom, Plato would be happy even as a slave.

Plato's adventure was not as dangerous as it might seem at first. In fact, it was just about paying the appropriate ransom. Since

Plato was known to be a wealthy man, a rather high sum was certainly demanded. It was paid by a certain Anniceris, a Greek from Libya. He had found himself in Aegina by accident on his way to Olympia to participate in the games which were to be held there for the 98th time [388 BC]. Anniceris intended to race four of his horses, which proves that he was very wealthy. It is doubtful whether he had known Plato before. The redemption of the philosopher from captivity was most likely a commercial transaction, and the benefactor was later reimbursed in full, with interest and guaranteed by Plato's friends.

After several more hours of sailing, Plato finally found himself in his native land. He had visited many lands and had gained a lot of experience.

THE 98ᵗʰ OLYMPICS

Plato's liberator, Anniceris, landed on the shores of the Peloponnese and proceeded to Olympia from there. We do not know whether his team was successful. However, we do know that the horses of the tyrant of Syracuse, Dionysius, did not win anything that year, which must have greatly pleased Plato.

The tyrant had sent several teams of horses to Olympia. The great Syracusan embassy was led by his brother, Thearidas, the commander of the fleet and the second-highest ranking person in the state. The embassy made a showing of incredible splendor. The greatest admiration was aroused by their gilded tents laid with precious carpets. The Olympic team included a group of excellent singers sent to perform the poems of Dionysius.

However, fate did not favor the Syracusans.

The trouble began with an argument over the fundamental question of whether it was lawful to admit Dionysius' men to the games at all. The view that they should not be admitted was advanced by Lysias. It was the same Lysias who, fifteen years earlier, when Athens had been ruled by the Commission of Thirty, lost all fortune;

whose brother Polemarch was executed; and who only saved himself by escaping miraculously through the back gate of the house where he had been imprisoned. After the fall of the Thirty, Lysias returned to Athens and became famous as a lawyer, but he never recovered his lost fortune.

And now Lysias attacked Dionysius before the immense crowds gathered in Olympia. He argued that the henchmen of a tyrant should not be allowed to profane with their presence the sacred games of free men. He called for Sicily to be freed from the yoke of the autocrat. He felt entitled to speak for Syracusans because his family had come from Syracuse, having settled in Athens only two generations earlier and at the urging of Pericles himself. We have heard that story here from Cephalus, the father of Lysias.

Lysias succeeded in stirring up his audience. There was a riot, and the magnificent tents of the Syracusans were plundered and destroyed. But the teams sent by Dionysios took part in the competition. They were not successful: some ran off the track, while others bumped into each other. Nor did Dionysius triumph in the poetic competition, despite the beauty of his singers' voices.

It is clear that Dionysius's participation in the Games and Lysias's strident opposition to it had political ramifications. The ruler of Syracuse wanted to dazzle Hellenes with his power, while Lysias fought for a great and noble cause. He managed to present to the Greeks, who had come to Olympia from many lands, the catastrophic situation in which their homeland had found itself. The core of his argument, as far as the surviving fragments allow us to reproduce it, went like this:

A new fratricidal war has been raging in Greece for seven years. Its staggering cost has prompted various Greek states to take Persian money. As a result, Greek cities in Asia Minor have fallen the Persian yoke, and the ships of the King of Kings reappeared in the Aegean Sea. And what is happening in the West? The tyrant of Syracuse, mighty on land and sea, subdues and destroys the Greek cities of Sicily and now threatens even Italy. And in this way, Hellas, feuding and weak, found herself between two superpowers which have but one objective in common: to deprive Greece of her freedom.

Lysias cried:

The woeful misfortune of our brothers, who have already been enslaved, is our misfortune. Shall we wait passively until the two autocrats, the King of Kings and the Tyrant of Syracuse, join hands and strike directly at us? We must unite our strength and resist their arrogant self-confidence together!

Thus, Lysias rose above the petty particularisms of most citizens of small city-states. And he was probably able to do it because he was a citizen of none: his family had come from Syracuse, and while his home was in Athens, that city had confiscated his property and denied him any political rights. And yet, somehow, these personal defeats seemed to free Lysias and to allow him to see the bigger political picture.

He called for the unity of all Hellenic states. He called for the reconciliation of the two mortal enemies—Athens and Sparta. He believed that this was the only way to save what was most precious: the political independence of all of Greece and the political liberties of all Greeks. But how many contemporary Hellenes were able to think in similar terms? I'm not sure that even Plato understood the danger of the situation. I certainly do not find in his writings any hint of the awareness that the political existence of Hellas was coming to an end.

HELLAS BETWEEN EAST AND WEST

Yet, it had to be obvious to the more discerning minds that a new political configuration was taking shape, and the threat of a great alliance was emerging: an alliance of Persia, Lacedaemon, and Syracuse. This was evidenced by two facts: Lacedaemonians were negotiating with Persians, and at the same time, the Lacedaemonian envoy Pollis stayed with Dionysius in Syracuse.

In his speech, Lysias suggested what the future might hold in store, but he didn't recommend any countermeasures. Perhaps he couldn't—perhaps none were possible. And who knows if the violence of his attack did not worsen the situation by unleashing passions and inciting the mob to riot. The plundering and destruction of the tents in Olympia infuriated Dionysius and probably prompted him to undertake a decisive demonstration of his power the following year.

The Lacedaemonian government had by then concluded a treaty with the king of Persia, by the terms of which all Greek cities on Cyprus and in Asia Minor would become Persian subjects, and all others were to be left free to live in peace and to govern themselves by their own laws. Lacedaemon undertook to enforce the terms, and the King of Kings to guarantee them. In other words, Lacedaemonians sold their brethren in Asia Minor to the Persians and, in return, gained the honorable task of maintaining Hellas as a collection of weak, quarreling states.

Athens, however, still had a large navy at its disposal, and she was not ready to bow to the will of Persia and Lacedaemon. And at this crucial moment, Dionysius stepped in. A strong Syracusan squadron joined the Lacedaemonian navy in the Aegean Sea. The combined forces threatened to cut off the lifeline of Athens: the trade routes leading to the Black Sea. Athens had to yield and humbly accept the peace, rightly called the Royal Peace. Within a few months, the peace was adopted and sworn by all the leading states of Hellas: Corinth, Athens, Thebes.

And now, there really was no more point involving oneself in politics anymore. Even Plato must have seen it.

THE SHORTEST ROUTE TO THE BEST SYSTEM

This is what they taught us in Athens:

After returning from Sicily, Plato purchased a piece of land near the sacred Grove of Academus,[35] just outside the city walls. There he established a religious association in honor of the Muses. This foundation, which also functions as a school, has been a place of lectures and disputes ever since. It has survived over five centuries, despite so many upheavals, wars, and cataclysms. I believe with all my heart that it will withstand future storms, also. Perhaps the Academy will not remain in the same place. Perhaps it will choose to transfer to another city. And who knows if there will not be many such Academies in the future. But they will all be daughters of this mother.[36]

For the next twenty years, Plato remained in Athens. He wrote and taught. He wanted to gather around him and educate virtuous and wise men who would be able, when a favorable moment presented itself, to establish and lead the perfect political system of which he constantly dreamed. For although he was seemingly not interested in current political events, the passions of his youth did not die out completely. Why do I say that? Suffice it to say that it was then that he began to write *The Republic*, in which he describes in great detail the constitution of the ideal state as he saw it.

But we have other evidence, too. After twenty years, an urgent summons came from Syracuse. Dionysius had died. His son, Dionysius II, aged about thirty, took power. His uncle, Dion, so well known to Plato from an earlier time, was now very influential in Syracuse. It was probably his idea to invite Plato, and Plato accepted the invitation with alacrity. It seems that Dion had hinted that excellent perspectives were opening in Syracuse, perspectives of putting Plato's political ideas into practice.

---

[35] Academus was said to have saved Athens from an attack by Sparta, by revealing where Helen of Troy was hidden after she had been kidnapped by King Theseus (this happened before the incidents of the later Trojan War). Having thus spared Athens a war (or at least delayed it), Academus was seen as a savior of Athens. His property, north of Athens, became revered even by neighboring city-states, and escaped the destruction of the many local wars.

[36] The writer of these words held a chair of history at the Jagiellonian University, established in 1364.

The young Dionysius seems to have been a very gifted man and genuinely interested in philosophy. He inherited from his father not only power but also a lively intelligence, the desire to surround himself with great minds, and—literary ambition. Plato—by then already famous—was to constitute the most precious gem in the Syracusan crown.

The philosopher set to work immediately: he began to write *The Laws*, the book which I have often quoted here already. These laws were to become the basis of that perfect political system to be founded in Sicily under the rule of young Dionysius. Right there, in the fourth book of the work, the interlocutors discuss a very important question:

"In what country will it be easiest to introduce our laws?"

And the answer is:

"Give us a country ruled by a tyrant! If only he is young, talented, brave, and magnanimous."

Dionysius II seemed to possess all these attributes, and the last sentence is a clear nod to him. I am tempted to say that the flattery is a tad overdone. But the thesis—"Give us a tyrant!"—brings honor to Plato's insight. For indeed, speaking practically and realistically: most people are ignorant and do not understand where their good and happiness lie. Therefore it will be necessary to use force to lead them there, reluctant and unwilling, at least at first. And there is no constitution that gives a prudent shepherd more power than tyranny does.

I believe I wrote somewhere above that "No thought ever dies." Somewhere, someday each thought may become a reality. For ideas, as Plato teaches, are eternal and immutable; and therefore, so is the idea concerning the shortest path to the best political system.[37]

---

[37] This text, first published in 1970, was written under communism which promised to use the political tools of dictatorship ("dictatorship of the people") to lead its subjects to a better future. (Translator's note).

THE RULER AND HIS PHILOSOPHER

Dionysius was, of course, too prudent a ruler to take his guest's political fantasies seriously. He probably limited his reaction to *The Laws* to the grateful acknowledgment of the thesis that tyranny was the best way to the future happiness of the whole society. (How could he not?) All the same, he treated Plato with great hospitality because philosophy fascinated him. Alas, one of the court factions began to spread the rumor that Dion was plotting against the *strategos-autocrator* and planned to seize power for himself. The tyrant believed it, and Dion had to go into exile. This touched Plato very painfully. And yet he had to remain in Syracuse another year and a half.

When he finally returned to Athens, he found Dion there, for the Syracusan had taken up residence in the city and started frequenting the Academy. In those years, many eminent personalities from various cities of Hellas gathered in the Academy's porticoes and gardens, and the institution, today a quiet sanctuary of theoretical deliberations, resembled at the time a revolutionary cell plotting political upheavals across the Greek world.[38]

Five years passed, devoted to studies, discussions, and writing. And again, there came an urgent summons from Syracuse. Dionysius had truly cherished Plato and longed to have him back. It seems that the tyrant tried to assemble around him all the most interesting minds of his times—perhaps to play with them just as he played with the works of art which he collected on a vast scale. However, this time Plato refused firmly.

In response, the ruler sweetened his offer: he promised that if the philosopher came, he would pardon Dion. Thus, motivated by friendship, Plato set foot on Sicilian soil for the third time.

As was to be expected, the tyrant did not keep his promise— he had probably never intended to permit Dion to return. And when Plato insisted on Dion's return, he got into trouble himself. He

---

[38] A kind of Lumumba University

escaped from Syracuse and came to Athens only thanks to the intercession of powerful friends, in particular, the Pythagoreans of Taranto.

For the next twelve years, the founder of the Academy remained in his native city—until his dying day; and he died in the first year of the 108th Olympiad [348 BC] at the age of eighty or a little over eighty. Apparently, death came to him suddenly, during a wedding feast at the house of one of his friends.

Perhaps the second and third Sicilian voyages were more dramatic and more important than the first one (the visit with Dionysius I). And perhaps it would be proper to describe the fate of Dion, which was very turbulent. (He returned to Sicily still during Plato's lifetime, fought against Dionysius with varying luck, and finally died murdered by one of his friends, probably a student of the Academy).

But my thoughts keep coming back to Plato's first stay in Syracuse. It was then that his contacts with the Syracusan court were established, and that Dion fell under his influence. Both subsequent voyages were only the effect and the continuation of the first, and both were motivated by the same idea: to establish a perfect system with the help of a tyrant, for I am convinced that the philosopher was still looking for a ruler he could use. That is, he, the thinker, wanted to use an autocrat only as an instrument for the realization of his noble ideals. While the other, the autocrat and ruler, treated the intellectual only as a toy and trinket, which he sometimes showed to the world, saying: look how cultured I am, how I sponsor artists, how I look after the development of science, philosophy, and literature.

In this way, they each tried to fool the other: the ruler and his philosopher.

MYSTIFICATIONS

No sooner had I written these words than I started having some doubts. After all, in the Seventh Letter, Plato clearly states that already during his first stay in Syracuse, when he first met Dion, he had unconsciously started working towards the destruction of tyranny. It seems to follow that Plato's views changed significantly between his first and the second voyages to Syracuse, at least on one point: originally, he was an enemy of autocracy, but later he came to the conclusion that tyranny was an indispensable tool on the way to the ideal political system.

Or perhaps we can try to explain this inconsistency in another way:

Plato wrote the Seventh Letter at the end of his life, that is, after three journeys to Sicily and after many sad experiences with the rulers of Syracuse. And so perhaps, recalling his first visit in that letter, he attributed to his younger self views which he had not originally held. That is, he painted himself as opposed to tyranny from the first encounter with it, and he probably thought he had been. And thus, he committed a hoax—though I guess he did it unconsciously. How often we all do this: project our noble and wise intentions only belatedly born onto the past—when we wish we had had them.

However, this does not exclude the possibility of still another and far more serious hoax. Namely:

The Seventh Letter, as I have already said, is commonly regarded as Plato's work—a kind of autobiography. But is this so certain? After all, you could propose, and even try to prove, that the letter was written by someone else, living a little later, perhaps one of the master's disciples: someone sincerely interested in presenting Plato as a fearless fighter for freedom and an enemy of autocracy. For many minds, the contacts of the founder of the Academy with tyrants, widely known and commented upon, were an unpleasant stain on his reputation. And it would have been easiest to remove this stain by forging a letter like the Seventh Letter.

Such a person would then argue that what Plato had written about tyranny in the fourth book of *The Laws*—where he says that tyranny is the best way to achieve the perfect political system—should be regarded as meaningless because those are only the views of one of several fictitious people in a fictitious dispute and do not represent Plato's views at all.

This last case, if true, would solve another difficulty which I have mentioned already:

The author of the Seventh Letter strongly condemns the Thirty Tyrants, though he does not mention them by name. Whereas in the dialogues of Plato, two of the Thirty—Critias and Charmides—appear often and are warmly remembered as men worthy of respect.

And if this is so, if the Seventh Letter is indeed a forgery, was I right to take it as the point of departure in my study of the life and ideas of Plato? Was I fooled by a forgery? But what else could I have done? We simply do not have any other information about the founder of the Academy apart from the few fragments I have presented here. I would also add that this uncertainty, this vagueness of data, was a strong element of the appeal of my work. This groping around in the dark, in a world in which it is not clear what is fact and what is fiction feels somehow extraordinary, exciting, and beautiful: a true intellectual adventure!

And these reflections have given rise to new ideas about myself and my own situation. I shall have to defend myself in court soon—that much is clear. Emilianus and Pudens will make the accusation that I used black magic to ensnare and marry the richest woman in Oea. They will present a lot of evidence and call many witnesses. They will say:

"Apuleius hid mysterious items in his linen bundle! He used to buy strange, rare fish! He gave Tallus an attack of epilepsy! He ordered an image of a skeleton from a woodcarver! In the house of Crassus, he performed terrifying rites! He contributed to the death of Pontianus!"

I will appear before the tribunal. I will refute those accusations and prove their groundlessness. I will mock the ignorance of my accusers, and I will expose the dirt of their private lives. Finally, I will invoke the final argument: I will have Pudentilla's will read out, in which she appoints Pudens as her principal heir, and I am left only a very modest bequest. I will call the gods to witness that Pudentilla, angry with her son, wrote that will reluctantly and only yielding to my persuasion. And I will make it plain that in the new situation, in view of the lawsuit brought against me by Pudens, I will be unlikely to raise in myself sufficient enthusiasm to push for a similar version of the testament to be made.

If Pudentilla's will were to be read in court, it would have to be opened and the seals broken, and the document would thereby lose all legal force. A new one would then have to be prepared. And perhaps no one will be surprised if it should turn out—after many, many years of Pudentilla's happy conjugal life—that her new will should contain provisions quite different from her earlier will. For it just might happen that I will be appointed the principal heir to a lady worth four million.

I do not know, Dear Reader, where you happen to live—in what era, country, or political system. I don't know what your views, financial status, or education are. But because you have taken this little book in your hand and have been kind enough to read it this far, I suppose that you are no stranger to the questions of philosophy. Perhaps you even consider yourself a student of Plato, as I do. And if so, then tell me, Brother-Philosopher, tell me openly and honestly: for the sake of four million sesterces, would you not engage in a little harmless sorcery or commit a petty hoax?

What I have done, I leave to your imagination.

THE END

TRANSLATOR'S SPECIAL REQUEST

Translating and publishing this book has been a labor of love for me.
I grew up reading it, and I have always wanted to be able
to share it with my American friends. And so here it is.
It will not make me rich, but if you liked the book, would you please
recommend it to a friend?
And give it an Amazon review?
https://www.amazon.com/dp/2919820494

THANK YOU!

ABOUT THE AUTHOR

Aleksander Krawczuk (1922-2023) was a noted scholar of Greek and Roman antiquity, a professor at the Jagiellonian University, a former minister of culture, and an author of over 30 popular and widely translated books on the subject of the Antique.

ABOUT MONDRALA PRESS

Mondrala Press publishes English translations of great Polish books—books with a track record of international critical and commercial success but which, for political reasons, have never been published in English.
To see our newest titles or to subscribe
to our mailing list, please visit
www.mondrala.com
THE GREATEST BOOKS YOU HAVE NEVER HEARD OF

Seven Against Thebes

Before the Trojan War, there was the Theban War. Who fought it? Why? What does archeology tell us, and what has survived of ancient the epics?

The Last Olympiad

Serapeum destroyed! Emperor murdered! Pagans raise a revolt! Read leading lights of their time (389-395 AD) as they debate everything from bathing to demon possession.

A Meeting in Oea

Meet Apuleius, Rome's all-time best-selling author, a Platonic scholar, a part-time magician, and a dowry-hunter, as he works on his treatise on Plato at night and schemes to marry a rich African widow by day.

Titus and Berenice

The last vestiges of the kingdom of Judah hung for a while on the outcome of the love affair between the elderly Jewish queen Berenice, granddaughter of Herod the Great, and the 12 years younger son of Vespasian, the emperor of Rome.

Jacek Bocheński

Tiberius Caesar

Terror is normal.
The horrifying tale of Tiberius Caesar, the second emperor of Rome:
the man who normalized political terror. A moral, intellectual,
emotional zero whose only skill in life was to grab and hang onto
power. At any cost. A dizzying look into
the great void of an empty soul.

Joe Alex

The Ships of Minos 1-5

A Bronze Age Saga.
1600 BC. A Minoan ship sails to the ends of the earth in search of the
sources of amber. Days without night, water turning to stone, monsters of
the deep, peoples who sacrifice their kings to their gods and build great
stone circles to worship the sun. And god's face upon the waters.
One of the greatest exploration sagas ever written.

Arkady Fiedler

The White Jaguar 1-5

AD 1726. An uninhabited Caribbean island off the Spanish Main. A Virginian renegade. Pirates, Runaway slaves. Cannibals.
The great saga of the mysterious White Jaguar, a white man named John who became a war leader of the Orinoco Indians in their wars against the Spanish.

Maria Rodziewiczówna

A Summer of the Forest Folk

The most beautiful book you will read this year.
Turn of the nineteenth century. Three women spend their summers in a remote cottage deep in the last virgin forest in Europe. This summer, their teenage big-city nephew joins them. A heart-warming, feel-good tale of love and friendship, of coming of age, and of the healing power of nature. This is a book like nothing you have ever read, a phenomenon, a genre of its own.

Witold Makowiecki

Out of the Lion's Maw

570 B.C. They slip their jailors in Carthage and rush across the Mediterranean pursued by enemy agents and assassins: a mysterious oriental priest and his Greek apprentice. Their mission: to prevent the outbreak of a civil war in Egypt. Their opponents: the Great Phoenician Council and the entire state apparatus of Eternal Egypt. Their resources: the old man's wit and the young man's courage.

Wind from the Hospitable Sea

Greece 562 BC. For insolvent debtors, the price of bankruptcy is slavery. When his mother and siblings are seized for unpaid debts, little Diossos must run to fetch help. He must cross mountains, forests, and stormy seas, brave wild animals, slave catchers, pirates, and... the law. He has one month to achieve his quest but only days to grow up.